SCENES FROM THE PAST: 10

RAILWAYS IN AND ARO

BOLTON

An Historical Review

C000246572

Bolton East Junction, 26th July 1963   *Photo: P. Reeves*

by

BILL SIMPSON

Copyright © Bill Simpson & Foxline Publishing
ISBN 1 870119 11 8
All rights reserved
Designed and edited by Gregory K. Fox
Typeset by Ryburn Typesetting Ltd, Luddendenfoot, Halifax
Printed by The Amadeus Press Ltd, Huddersfield

Published by Foxline Publishing
32, Urwick Road, Romiley, Stockport, SK6 3JS

Preface

It would be impossible for me to write on the railways of Bolton without experiencing a sense of autobiography. As an infant I was cradled in Windley Street and perhaps the vibrations of those heavy freight trains climbing on the viaduct high above Folds Road made some impression on my slumbers, because I never ceased to feel some kind of affinity with them.

In fact the line to Blackburn and the Pennine reaches formed a continuous thread that paralleled my own development. By the time I had reached the age of regular dirty knees I was watching the passenger trains roar by, or so they seemed to do then, on a footbridge near Harry Peers Steelworks.

Further up the line I went to school and finally succumbed to the opiate of fascination for the railways. Not only the stunning grandeur of steam locomotives with their iconic impressiveness but the entire elaborate system of journies and destinations. This was vividly witnessed on a busy day at Trinity Street Station with its superbly elevated footbridge that provided a unique view, often concealed in dense white vapour as some locomotive hurled its plume of impatience from the safety valves a few feet beneath.

The sharpest etched recollections, probably because of the extra layer of excitement, are associated with holidays and 'Wakes Week'. Were the Fylde coast towns, north Wales and for the more adventurous – Bournemouth, all we needed? Indeed they were, and approached with great relish as the crowds tumbled down the station steps onto the platform with every size and weight of suitcase being dragged along with children and buckets and spades. The trains seemed to find effortless pathways close to this mass as all the doors of the carriages sprung open with the sheer force of anticipation, hardly before it stopped.

Far from the frisson of holiday week the large marshalling yards continued the habit of the working week with the endless lifting and hauling of the town's manufacture. Through the night the stubby little shunting engines ran back and forth; Burnden Junction, Crook Street yard, Bullfield, Halliwell and Astley Bridge. To a youngster lying in bed the odd acoustic sensation of the soft pulse of the exhaust, the clank of buffers and the release of the shunters pole seeming to take place on the rising mound of my pillow instead of two or three miles away in town.

In compiling and writing this book these are the experiences and memories always at the back of my mind, whilst present research has provided me with an insight that I never achieved in those far off days. Nevertheless, they remain with a richness beyond currency, when a pencil and cheap notebook was all that was required with the priceless gift of seeing. For this my gratitude to Bolton and the area around it covered by this book will remain for ever undiminished.

Bill Simpson
Banbury, 1990

Below: Bolton Great Moor Street, c.1926. Always playing second fiddle to its nearby neighbour in Trinity Street, this period view of the towns 'other' station possibly highlights the role to which it perhaps it was better suited, that of providing facilities for leisure travel, particularly to North Wales. Even after withdrawal of local services in 1954 it continued to serve for excursion traffic and the annual fortnightly 'wakes' period.

Photo: courtesy A. Smith

Historical Summary

Bolton's role in the history of railways has never received the prominence it deserves, probably due to being overshadowed by contemporary historical tableaux like Stockton & Darlington Railway and the Liverpool and Manchester Railway which are acknowledged landmarks in railway development. Nevertheless Bolton industrialists showed no lesser zeal in promoting a line and actually had it in business before the Liverpool and Manchester by two years.

By the time of the invention of Crompton's spinning mule in 1779 Bolton was already forming the nucleus of an industrial population. The exploitation of the local coalfields and the huge steam powered mills ensured its population expansion as more and more people gave up agricultural occupations and turned to the manufacture of yarn. Large families with working children could triple their income by moving to the town. Besides cotton operatives the industry needed the support of warehousemen, mechanics and stevedores. Gradually, Bolton became an important centre for bleaching, dyeing, printing and finishing. With the opening of the railways the population was well on its way to 50,000, a figure which had only been 10,000 in 1800.

Machines became the servants of the new order but the tyrants of the old for with Crompton's Mule came Kay's flying shuttle, its velocity mocking the patient fingers of thousands of hand-loom weavers. Their plight throughout the 1820's, 30's and 40's was of lengthening hours and of starvation amidst proliferating wealth.

As the rest of the country was waking up to 'Railway Mania' in the mid 1840's Bolton had nearly all its lines in operation with impressive connections to Manchester and Liverpool and another to Preston with only the line to Blackburn under construction, four centres of the great cotton boom that were all in their ascendancy. In 1820, before the building of the railway network, Lancashire exported 290 million yards of cloth. By 1860, with the core of the system complete, she exported 2,000 million. Other factors may well have prevailed to bring this about but the railways undoubtedly played a central role as 6,600 million yards was

reached by 1914. The staggering growth of Manchester bears witness to what was happening for in 1700 the population was 4,000, by 1841 it was 250,000, but ten years later with its main line railways open it had reached 400,000.

Fuel to all this production were the rich seams of coal around Wigan and Manchester, this analogous concentration needing only the railways to bring it to a rapidly expanding tempo. A railway from Liverpool to Manchester was under discussion as early as 1822, to foil in some way the virtual monopoly of trade by the powerful canal owners. Both goods and passengers were forced to use the Leeds–Liverpool Canal or venture on an indifferent road system. Bolton was also part of the canal system with the Bolton/Bury & Manchester Canal (1805) connecting twice daily with packet boats for both passengers and merchandise. The river and canal navigations were virtually forcing the railway to happen.

The merchants of the two large cities enlisted the services of the man of the hour, George Stephenson, to build such a railway and Bolton as an obvious partner in this trade triangle was not dilatory in realising this was the opportunity to grasp.

A number of leading manufacturers of Bolton, notably William Hulton, Benjamin Hick and Peter Rothwell, joined in forming a company called the Bolton and Leigh Railway. The times were risky and Stephenson had not been blooded on a truly major project, so the men wisely courted the canal interests at the same time by promoting the line not only having a station in Bolton, but to have a connection with the Bolton/Bury/ Manchester Canal near Great Lever and at the other end with the Leeds to Liverpool Canal at Leigh. At the same time a wary glance was kept on the progress of the Stephenson survey for the Liverpool & Manchester Railway as it passed through the committee stage of Parliament.

Stephenson was enlisted to do the Bolton and Leigh survey, which received its Act on the 31st March 1825, after the L & M Survey had received a derisory mauling. However, with a fresh approach, this railway achieved its Act in 1826.

1. Daubhill, c.1869. A remarkable view of a very early railway station, appropriately shown alongside Sunnyside Mills, Daubhill. The station is the first Daubhill station of the Bolton & Leigh at the top of the incline that was originally cable hauled. Buildings for the station appear to be at ground level on the mill side with waiting rooms alongside the low platform. The train just departing for Leigh and Kenyon Junction appears to be headed by an early 2-2-2. The massive signal and post is likely to have undergone some artistic license. After 1885, trains followed the diversionary route built on the other side of the mill and opened at that date. The area on each side of Barrier Street along which the horse and cart are proceeding became overlaid with the familiar gridiron of streets and terraced houses.

Photo: courtesy John Marshall

Unfortunately, this route brought the Liverpool & Manchester no closer to the Bolton & Leigh terminus at Leigh than Lowton, a little over two miles away.

The Bolton & Leigh opened their line of 7½ miles – which was freight only – on the 1st August 1828. As a public railway, this would mean carrying goods for local business interests either by company wagon or privately owned wagon.

A report in Bolton Chronicle describes a procession starting from Pendlebury Fold near Hulton Park where W. Hulton Esq. entertained a distinguished company with a luncheon or déjeuner.

Travelling from there they alighted at the top of the inclined plane whereupon the steam locomotive was named 'The Lancashire Witch'. The procession continued down the inclined plane but when passing under a bridge near Mr Carlisle's residence the crowd was so intense that several fell, one of these people being thrown down under the wheels of the last wagon, and suffering severe injuries.

It was planned that at the bottom of the hill the wagons would be attached to horses for the remainder of the journey but the populace insisted on pulling them by hand all the way to the terminus at Blackhorse Street. The estimation of the crowd was said to be about 40,000 and the weather was fine.

Bolton Chronicle announced on Saturday June 11th, 1831, that *The public are respectfully informed that the Bolton and Leigh Railway Co. will begin to convey passengers from Monday next the 13th inst. Coaches will start from Liverpool at a quarter before seven in the morning and two o'clock in the afternoon. Journeys from Bolton to Liverpool will start at ten o'clock and five-thirty. Fares: inside, 5 shillings, (25p) outside, three shillings and sixpence (17½ p).*

The apparent success of the Liverpool and Manchester tempted the Bolton interests to throw caution to the winds and ignore the canal involvement, necessary encouragement being received by the promotion of a Kenyon & Leigh Junction Railway Act of the 14th May 1829. On the 1st January 1831, this short but crucial section enabled the 9 miles 6 furlongs to Kenyon Junction to be opened for freight traffic.

The way was now clear not only to Liverpool and Manchester but to Warrington and north to Wigan and Preston. With such an early connection with this developing means of transport Bolton had tied herself in firmly with the destinies of the two most dynamic cities of the 19th century, their continuing enterprise and expansion of trade.

Furthermore, on the 11th June 1831, a passenger service was operating between Bolton and Kenyon Junction which would facilitate an interchange of the businessmen themselves across the triangle. The tiny Kenyon & Leigh was subsequently leased by B&L in 1836.

Returning to the details of the Bolton & Leigh, it is interesting to note the occupations of its promoters. Although the Cotton industry was well represented with twelve men of that business it was also balanced by eight ironfounders and two colliery owners. Bolton's dominating role in the cotton industry overshadowed the fact that the town had also held a long tradition in heavy engineering, a factor that to some degree obviated the

distress of the 1862 cotton famine that so blighted towns like Preston and Manchester.

The opening of the line reduced the price of coal by two shillings (10p) a ton in Bolton.

Promoters of the Bolton and Leigh.

John Mawdsley, Thomas Holmes, William Morris (Cotton manufacturers): Thomas Bolling, Edward Bolling, William Bolling (Spinners): Richard Ainsworth, Peter Ainsworth, George Blair (Bleachers): H Duckworth (Calico Printer); William Pratt, Richard Taylor (Reed Makers) etc, etc.

John Rainforth	(Vitriol and Bleaching Powder Manufacturers)
Joseph Cole	(Iron Founders)
Isaac Dobson	" "
Benjamin Dobson	" "
Benjamin Hick	" "
James Hilton	" "
Peter Rothwell	" "
William Swift	" "
Thomas Thompson	" "
William Hulton	(Colliery Owners)
John Booth	" "
Matthew Carr Dawes	(Brewer)
Ralph Spooner	(Manager & Engineer of Gasworks)
Will Bowker	(Merchant)
Will Tickle	"
James Tickle	"
Johnson Lomax	(Linen Draper)
James Gray	(Slate and Timber Merchants)
James Scowcroft	(Chemist)

Capital for the line was subscribed to £44,000 in £100 shares, whilst Stephenson's estimate was for £43,143. 1s. 0d (£43,143.05), detailed as follows:

	£	s	d
Excavations & embankments from Bolton to Toll bar	1765	1	0
From Toll bar to the top of the incline plane to Hulton Park	5162	12	8
From the inclined planes to the canal at Leigh	7303	8	8
Total	14231	2	4
Rails	8360	0	0
Remaining	20551	18	8
Total Estimate	43143	1	0

Not detailed are the two stationary engines which presumably would be paid for from the remaining total

2. Chequerbent, 8th June 1949. An excellent view of the Chequerbent incline as LMS built 4F No. 44356, of Warrington (Dallam) shed, attacks the 1 in 30 gradient on its way to Bolton. The effects of mining subsidence are said to have induced a 1 in 18 gradient in places. Not surprisingly, there were special instructions for the working of freight trains. Working the bank was difficult for crews, particularly as a 35 miles per hour limit was placed on trains whilst passing through Chequerbent station. On the occasion of this view there are only six wagons in tow, whereas if the total reached fifteen a banking engine had to be provided. The formation of the line nearby was ultimately breached by the M61 motorway, not even a planners dream when this photograph was taken. The town of Atherton provides a backdrop. *Photo: W.S. Garth*

In trying to imagine the Bolton of the late 1820's that received the first railway one needs to disregard a great deal of nineteenth century and some twentieth century development. Beyond a half mile radius of the town centre, places like Deane, Halliwell, Sharples and Tonge Moor were all remote country villages and hamlets.

As with other Lancashire towns the forty years or so from 1830 would see a staggering growth of industry only checked in some measure by the cotton famine of 1861–2.

By 1926 when the town was bristling with chimneys of cotton mills the last building of the great age of iron and cloth culminated in the opening of Sir John Holden's Mill at Astley Bridge.

Bolton's motto 'Supera Moras' must have seemed more of an ideal than a reality to George Stephenson as he surveyed the railway to Leigh and the daunting gradient required for the climb to Daubhill before attaining the level he needed capable of using his steam locomotives on. Although Rainhill saw the feted entree of the locomotive it was some time before it attained a bulkier grandeur, early engines looking more like steam perambulators that needed kinder landscapes. Thus, the stationary engine and cable haulage was to play a prominent role on the Bolton & Leigh for at least fifteen years, producing an interesting example, amongst the few, of the transitional years embodying both techniques.

Starting its 7¾ miles from a place called Lecturers Closes, virtually at the foot of Derby Street, the steam engine of 20 hp drew the cable wagons to the summit at Daubhill (Deane Church Lane) up a hefty 1 in 33, before continuing by means of locomotive haulage – the first an 0-4-0 called *Lancashire Witch* – to the downward incline at Chequerbent, where the second steam engine, this time of 50 hp, took over on a little kinder but lengthier 1 in 55 gradient. Colliery subsidence in later years would convert this to a punishing 1 in 18 section, bringing it close to being the steepest adhesion worked gradient in the country – Hopton incline on the Cromford and High Peak was 1 in 14 – it is believed that the stationary engines remained to about 1846.

With the introduction of the passenger service, stations were located at Bolton, Daubhill, Chequerbent, Atherton, West Leigh and Pennington. The Station at Bolton was little more than a shed with a booking office whilst at Kenyon Junction there was a porter's lodge and a waiting room.

One of the leading promoters of the B & L was William Hulton, a colliery owner, whose coal mining interests near Chequerbent would feature prominently in the history of this line. From the beginning on the celebrated opening day, wagons carrying his coal descended the incline and were distributed charitably. One hundred and thirty six years later a string of wagons from a Hulton colliery bearing the initials NCB (National Coal Board) would be the last load bearing vehicles to regularly use the line.

Coal and cotton formed the essential alliance of progress and Hulton's collieries amalgamated their interest with local industrial demand bringing in some 60,000 tons per annum at the opening of the B & L. Some local pits sunk their shafts very deep, going to 1,000 feet, whilst Parsonage Colliery at Leigh descended a staggering 4,000 feet into the earth, a darkness greater than the mere extinction of light. The hazard of mining could not be more grimly illustrated than the explosion at the Hulton Colliery Pretoria Pit, at Chequerbent on the 21st December 1910, when 344 men and boys suffered death from a ghastly conflagration whose proportions are so tellingly obvious in such a massive loss of life. The holly and the ivy wore a sombre hue in local villages that Christmastide, especially Westhoughton.

Another leading promoter of the line, Benjamin Hick, has left his memorial in the form of the still productive works of Hick, Hargreaves. The founders of this company were very prominent in the nineteenth century well beyond the borough boundaries. Engines by Hick & Rothwell included a vertical boiler locomotive for the Bolton & Leigh in 1830. They also produced locomotives in 1851 for the Bristol and Exeter Railway, 9ft 4-2-4 tanks and many others. The works of Rothwell, Hick Union Foundry was situated on Moor Lane, a large warehouse abutting onto Deansgate and served by a long siding from the goods yard of the B&L that ran through Ormrod Street and over New Street before reaching these works, the warehouse and coal depot. The works eventually became Bolton Iron & Steel Company in about 1860 and for a period from 1866–71 F.W. Webb, the celebrated locomotive engineer of the London and North Western Railway, was the works manager. In 1906 it was taken over by Henry Bessemer & Co Ltd, and continued trading under that name until 1926 when it was demolished. The siding through the streets that served it was lifted shortly afterwards. The Deansgate warehouse lasted until February 25th 1930 before closure but the building remained until demolition in the late 1970's.

Hargreave's illuminating career began with large scale hiring out of vehicles to local merchants to carry their goods on the new railway, thus allowing private owner vehicles on exactment of a toll to the company.

The railways were still largely under the trading influence of the canal system. Hargreaves owned 200 vehicles that were mostly covered and of superior design for their day and were much sought after. 'Going by Hargreaves' became a common phrase among local merchants.

Closer to the goods yard and alongside the branch at Crook Street was the Soho Foundry which was started by Benjamin Hick when he left Peter Rothwell on Moor Lane in 1833 to start his own works. His son William Hick went into partnership with John Hargreaves after Benjamin Hick's death in 1842, thus Hick, Hargreaves was formed. John Hick, William's son, became a director of the LNWR and subsequently had a class of three-cylinder compound locomotive named after him.

With regard to passenger working, the B& Lhad two coaches for first class passengers that were identified with the Bolton coat of arms, one being called 'Elephant', and the other 'Castle'. Second and third class passengers tended to have very uncoachlike vehicles. The journey commenced from Bolton at 6.45am, arriving at Liverpool at 8.25am, a creditable 1 hr 40 mins for the journey. Another followed at 2pm, return workings were 10am and 5.30pm and for this priviledge first class passengers were charged 5 shillings (25p) inside and 3 shillings (15p) outside. The fare included a horse drawn omnibus from Dale Street to the railway terminus at Crown Street, Liverpool.

Engines used for this service were *Sans Pareil* (borrowed from L & M), *Union* (of Rothwell, Hick Foundry, Bolton), *Salamander and Vetran* (by Crook & Dean of Bolton). The engine and train of Union attained the 'Blue Riband' by reaching the speed of 35 mph along some sections of the route, doubtless the famous Dr Lardner's hypothesis of the expiration of human life beyond 30 mph had not reached north country ears.

The existence of the Bolton & Leigh Company was not destined to be long, for it had been one of the very earliest of the small companies with only modest capital and so its continued development would require its involvement in a larger scheme of things. By an Act of 1845 the B&L, K&LJ and L&M were merged with the Grand Junction Railway. In the following year this company was itself amalgamated with the Manchester and Birmingham and London and Birmingham Railways to form the London and North Western Railway, therefore on the 1st July 1846, the station in Bolton became Bolton LNWR.

Little was changed to the established order of things in the first few years until a drama of wider consequences was enacted in the dark morning of the 28th January 1858 at 6.35am.The nature of Bolton's first railway would be a problem for engines with the discontinuing of cable haulage, as Trevithick 2-4-0 side tank No. 156 *Redstart* discovered when from North Daub Hill with 18 loaded coal wagons and 14 filled with general merchandise. It is not clear whether the enginemen knew the road very well or had suffered a temporary lapse from regulations, for it was essential in the extreme to ensure that the train be halted at the top of the incline with the brakes of every other wagon pinned down before descending. The hapless *Redstart* was not afforded this advantage before continuing its jouney to the goods yard with the inevitable conclusion. As the train rattled down the gradients of 1 in 48 and 1 in 54, its speed gathered apace, producing a roar that could be heard in the yard at Bolton leaving little doubt to the workmen standing there of what was happening. Fortunately, they took the necessary precautions for their safety and ensured that the casualty list was kept to a minimum. The train smashed through the level-crossing gates on Crook Street and continued at some considerable speed into the station where it ran into a line of empty coaches, propelling them into some stone pillars and supports of the station buildings which were demolished to leave little else intact until it was arrested by the rubble it had created, standing useless amongst its own escaping vapours. The local press reported that the scene of devastation was beyond description with rubble, trucks of spilled coal, smashed coaches and building materials strewn over a wide area. The only fatality was a luckless railway worker, a platelayer, who had joind the train at Atherton and rode on the footplate with driver Richard Rigby and Stoker William Nuttall, both of whom jumped clear when they realised their fate. George Royle was found dead jammed against a pipe in the front of the engine.

Whatever conclusions were drawn in the Euston boardroom regarding the accident, it must have been obvious that an inherited feature of defunct cable working was bound to be a continuing hazard.

It seems certain that temporary arrangements must have been made at Bolton in the light of what had happened, whilst guidelines were drawn up as to how the new station would be built and in what form.

The expansion of the Hulton family interests in the district coincided with a proposed line by the LNWR from Manchester to Wigan, resulting in the Eccles Junction and Springs Branch route opened on the 1st September 1864. Forming a junction with the ET&W at Roe Green, a short branch to Little Hulton was built together with a mineral line to Hanging Bank Colliery. It was then decided to extend the branch into Bolton which brought into being a totally new and splendidly designed terminal station to take not only Liverpool–Leigh–Bolton trains but those from what became Manchester (Exchange) as well. The new Bolton station, following the classic 'Italian' style, was elevated above Great Moor Street with a bridge over Crook Street. The goods yard remained at street level. The station was opened for goods to Manchester on 16th November, 1874 whilst a passenger service was introduced along this route on the 1st of the following April, new stations being provided at Walkden, Little Hulton and Plodder Lane.

Having substantially modified the situation of the terminus, the LNWR began to take in hand matters concerning the B&L route. A Widening and Improvements Act was realised in July 1878 which meant in reality that the gradient would be eased by completely circumnavigating the former cable haulage section on a wider arc and alignment and the doubling of the track of the route through to Kenyon Junction. In effect two sections of the old route at each end remained as sidings, at Daubhill for coal and at Bridgeman Street for trains of Burton water for Magee Marshalls Brewery. The old line at Daubhill continued for many years to hold up traffic at Derby Street as locomotives and wagons rumbled across.

All of the new work had been completed by the 2nd February, 1885. The old site of Daubhill station was resited from the bottom of Barrier Street to the junction of Deane Church Lane and Derby Street. Situated above a cutting, the station had glazed stairwalks to the platforms and was an example of uniform style that the railways were developing, the intention being that one company's style would be familiar from one end of the system to the other. There was much modular timber construction in railway workshops transported to the site by train. This method of building differentiated stations from the early period when ad hoc assemblies were carried out by local contactors who may have been just builders with little or no railway experience putting up a building for a small local company, economically justified by the most convenient supply of local materials. Many early Bolton stations were contrived in this manner and built in the local stone.

As long as railway mileage was high in the district the developing web of local lines were prosperous, especially on the goods side. This secure trade pathway followed innocently and not a little complacently up to the cataclysm of the first world war in 1914, the high point of the imperial world that was to shatter and carry with it many of its institutions.

A Rival Hand

During the protracted plans of the Bolton & Leigh, the site in Bolton called Lecturers Closes was also the site of its diversification. Whereas the main line continued to the terminus at Great Moor Street, another prong wound circuitously on its way of about a mile to the Deansgate warehouse whilst a third was to join the Manchester, Bolton & Bury Canal. Bearing in mind the fact that the canal was on a steeply lower elevation from the station area, this would be bound to need a further cable worked incline which probably did not appear, as events transpired, so attractive a prospect. The B&L had courted interests of the powerful canal lobby and then ignored it at Leigh, and it was to do the same at Bolton by dispensing with the notion of joining the afore mentioned waterway there.

Not surprisingly the canal owners were not likely to stand by in dead water and so promoted their own alternative, a direct line between Bolton and Manchester.

This second railway would tie Bolton more securely still to the trade capital of Manchester. It would also produce the embryo of another great company – the Lancashire and Yorkshire Railway.

The canal directors at first considered conversion of their waterway into a railway, a swift change of faith indeed. To this effect an Act was obtained in 1831 to stop up the canal from Manchester to Bolton and construct a railway on either side of the waterway. In 1832 the directors changed their minds and obtained an Act to alter the original scheme in order that a railway might be constructed by the side of the canal throughout its course. Three years later further alteration was made and a more direct route taken from Clifton to Bolton.

On Tuesday 29th May 1838, the line was opened for traffic from a terminus in New Bailey Street, Salford, to Bolton.

Such an early line had some variations in its track with some at 55lb per yard fixed to cast-iron pedestals, some on continuous longitudinal stone whilst others were attached to cross-timbers in the conventional way. The gauge was to the adopted Stephenson measurement of 4 ft 8½ inches.

Four engines were supplied to the company to the design of Edward Bury of the Clarence Foundry. They were named *Fairfield, Victoria, Bolton* and *Manchester*. Further motive power included machines made by George Forrester, these being *Forrester* and *Buck*, with William Fairbairn's *Windermere, Crosley, Woolton* and *Bootle* completing the list.

Stations on the new line from Salford were sited at Dixon Fold, Ringley and Moses Gate. Ringley became Stoneclough and Kearsley in 1894 and simply Kearsley in 1903. The station that became known as Farnworth and Halshaw Moor opened in 1845 whilst Dixon Fold had the distinction of becoming an early casualty by closing on 18th May, 1931.

A 295 yard tunnel at Farnworth was duplicated with a second bore alongside in December 1880, and then widened in anticipation of the Midland Railway, which had running rights over the line and through to its Carlisle route at Hellifield, introducing a Pullman service.

The *Bolton Chronicle* reported the opening day of the line with an enthusiasm that was to become very familiar in many publications throughout the country in the decade to follow.'*The train reached Bolton at about 26 minutes after 7 o'clock having performed the journey in about 24 minutes. There was a considerable concourse of people gathered on the high ground overlooking the line to witness the arrival of the train. Passengers ascend a flight of stairs wholly unconnected with the booking office then leave the station in Bradford Square opposite the tower of Trinity Church proceeding along Bradshawgate to the town. After arrival of the train a horse and coach proceeded to Manchester whilst the passengers on the next train for Manchester did not leave Bolton for upwards of an hour afterwards but were in Manchester before those that travelled by coach*'. Thus the *Chronicle* made the observation that was to ring the death knell for thousands of coach routes and unemployment for drivers, grooms and ostlers whilst the coach stations fell into decay and the roads silent. The *Chronicle* observations continue....'*The first train from Bolton was at 7am, it accomplished its journey in about 19½ minutes. The second train to leave, with two first class and three second class carriages, departed at 28 minutes before 9 o'clock carrying fifty-nine passengers. It reached New Bailey Street station at 7½ minutes before 9 o'clock*'. Mass movement had begun.

Offices for the new railway company were set up in Bridgeman Street where they announced their fare tarriffs of 1st Class 2s 6p (12½p), 2nd Class 2s 0d (10p) and children under seven years of age at half price.

Remarkable enterprise was shown in view of the primitive condition of early railways by advertising their special trains for Manchester Races shortly after opening. Courageously taking the view that if they were going to run a railway for profit at all they would have to take the bull by the horns and meet public demand. A day of what must have been the earliest excursion arrangements ran as follows:

'*Trains to run to Agecroft Bridge for the Manchester Races with closed carriages charge 1s 6d (7½p) and open at 1s 0d (5p) operating at a quarter of an hour service from 12 o'clock until 2.45pm. For the returning crowds they would operate a half-hourly service from Agecroft to Bolton from 4 o'clock every half hour until the race ground is cleared.*' Engines in use on the day: *Victoria, Fairfield, Manchester, Bolton, Forrester and Buck.*

In 1846 the Manchester & Bolton Railway was amalgamated with the Manchester & Leeds Railway, thus bringing about a trans-Pennine connection. Several other schemes were drawn into the same amalgam including three more Bolton lines and so in 1847 the Manchester & Leeds assumed the title of the Lancashire and Yorkshire Railway. It is interesting to recount that two Bolton companies were the genesis of two of the largest railways in the country, the LNWR and the LYR.

For virtually fifty years Bolton was an axis of trains between Liverpool and Manchester. The pressure of traffic and the need for a direct route ventured the LYR to build a new railway from Manchester via Pendleton to Hindley (with a branch to Blackrod), through Wigan and on to Liverpool. It also enabled trains for Preston and Southport to avoid Bolton. The line ran from Windsor Bridge and was open to Hindley on 1st October 1888, and to Blackrod on 1st June 1889. A link was also built from Brindle Heath Junction to Agecroft Junction to provide an alternative route through Pendleton Broad Street for trains between Manchester and Bolton.

A Prospect North – Bolton and Preston Railway

In the developing constellation of Lancashire towns, Preston's place was assured. As a dockland town at the mouth of the Ribble it was not destined to the international fame of Liverpool on the Mersey but it did serve as a second capital of north Lancashire as a gateway to the north and the Fylde coast towns.

As a cotton producer it was sprouting mills at the speed of other towns in the group and significantly it was placed on the route of the west coast main line to Scotland in 1838. To reach Preston from Bolton one needed to travel over the Liverpool and Manchester Railway to Parkside and then north by the North Union Railway, a total distance of 36 miles and somewhat circuitous.

To the men of Bolton a link with Preston seemed a natural proposal, materialising as an Act on 15th June 1837 whilst the Manchester and Bolton was under construction. The first section of the line from Bolton was opened as far as Rawlinson Bridge (9½ miles), on the 4th February 1839 with stage coaches completing the journey to Preston. Chorley was reached on 22nd December 1841 and there were intermediate stations at Lostock Lane, Horwich Road and Adlington. The line was opened throughout on the 22nd June 1843 after some haggling about the junction with the North Union at Euxton. The North Union station at Preston opened on 31st October 1838, running powers being neeeded for the last 5½ miles over their line.

It is interesting to note that some of the promotors of this line were also amongst the promotors of the Bolton & Leigh, namely Edward Bolling, Benjamin Dobson and Benjamin Hick, whilst the company chairman was no less a person than John Hargreaves. Not surprisingly, their proposal contained a branch connection with the Bolton & Leigh which did not materialise apart from a short lived siding from Great Moor Street Station to Bull Field.

As the new route was six miles shorter than the existing one, there was some intensive rate cutting between the North Union and the Bolton & Preston and when the North Union started to delay the rival trains the smaller company had to revert to threats of finding an alternative route by converting a canal into a railway for the contentious 5½ miles. After some financial horse trading the two companies amalgamated in January 1844 before passing shortly afterwards into the hands of the LNWR and LYR.

A New Route to Liverpool – The Liverpool & Bury Railway

The final connection to Bolton's reticular network of lines was this west–east link of 1845; Liverpool–Wigan–Bolton–Bury. This was in fact an attempt by the Manchester & Leeds to break the monopoly of the Liverpool and Manchester lines, which, by introducing an extension from Rochdale to Bury, could be achieved. Work began from Tithe Barn Street, Liverpool, in January 1846 and reached Lostock where it joined with the Bolton and Preston Railway (now owned by the North Union Railway) on the 20th November 1848. Passing through Bolton and over the metals of the existing Manchester line it turned east and crossed the Croal and Tonge Valleys on high viaducts, the first example of this type of engineering feature in the town. These were modified in 1860 to stone piers with lattice girder decking, said to be the first example of this construction in England.

Tithe Barn Street actually opened on the 13th May 1850. Its replacement, Liverpool Exchange, opened in July 1888, but was itself closed on Friday 29th April, 1977.

A station was opened at Chew Moor between Lostock Junction and Westhoughton but was closed in 1852.

'Up the Bank' – to Blackburn

Probably the most spectacular line out of Bolton was that to Blackburn which later became part of the 48¾ miles from Manchester to Hellifield, although its progress was somewhat piecemeal.

Looking north of Bolton beyond its rooftops, one unfailingly looks into a moorland landscape. This foot of the Pennine chain begins to rise almost from the town centre itself and gives no quarter to any railway going in that direction.

It was in 1845 that the Blackburn, Darwen and Bolton Railway drew their scheme. The Bolton & Leigh had abruptly taken their gradient in one great leap, but the moorland line was going to have to achieve its goal at 720 feet above that of the sea by sheer prolongued perspiration.

Construction began in September of 1845 from Blackburn, taking two years to cover the five miles to reach the summit of Cranberry Moss, a section which included the Sough Tunnel (2,015 yards) on a gradient of 1

in 74; that was on the 3rd August 1847. The remaining 9 miles to Bolton were completed on the 12th June, 1848 and included the 73 stone arch viaduct required to maintain a level and cross the Tonge Valley. A further four cast iron spans were needed to carry the railway over the Croal Valley, although there was some delay when a number of the stone spans collapsed in the summer and had to be rebuilt.

During its construction the railway became enjoined with the aspirations of the Blackburn, Clitheroe and North Western Railway. On July 9th, 1847, the opening day, saw the official name of the company as the Bolton, Blackburn, Clitheroe and West Yorkshire Railway, it was subsequently absorbed by the LYR in 1849.

First stations on the line were Sough, north of the tunnel which had a more lyrical relief for its dour association in 1870 when it became Spring Vale and Sough. After a further seven years the less appealing half of the name was dropped altogether and it became simply – Spring Vale. A station located south of the tunnel was temporarily call Whittlestone Head, closing after just two months and being renamed Entwistle. On moving south, other stations were at Chapel Town, which became Turton in 1877 and Turton and Edgeworth in 1891, and Bromley Cross, this latter being opened along with the original stations. The last before Bolton acquired a more sylvan association and was simply called 'The Oaks'.

In October 1880 as part of an agreement with the Midland Railway, which was planning to run Pullman Coaches on its Manchester–Scottish services, the track of Sough tunnel was lowered 15 inches to enable the greater clearances, work being finished by 17th February 1882. The Midland Railway incidentally had offices in Bolton at 98, Bradshawgate.

An added curiosity to the line was the building of a branch from the viaduct at Folds Road passing through Halliwell to Astley Bridge, a distance of just over a mile to a terminus alongside Blackburn Road. It opened on the 15th October, 1877 and was both proposed and built by the LYR. The developing tramway system in the town proved too competitive for the branch, which was probably never seriously considered for its passenger traffic, the result being that discontinuation of the passenger service became one of the curiosities of railway lore as it took place only two years later on the 1st October 1879. Henceforth it continued as a goods yard and coal depot, the sidings at Halliwell extended and greatly enlarged with a huge goods warehouse rivalling the facility in the town centre. Astley Bridge coal depot was closed in 1961 whilst Halliwell closed 3rd August 1981.

The main route gradually expanded to encompass the somewhat pompous latitude of its title, reaching Hellifield in 1880. Following the opening of the Settle and Carlisle route in 1876, the Midland sought, and obtained, running rights over what was by that time a Lancashire and Yorkshire line (BB & C and WYR being merged into that company in 1858) with their trains from and to Manchester and Scotland.

The Bolton area was not, by the furthest stretch of imagination, endowed with 'pretty' stations. They were all serviceable and boldly businesslike, in the manner of the giant mills that in many cases served as a backdrop. The most interesting group were those between Bolton and Sough tunnel, a series of squat rugged buildings, hewn from the local stone and blending well with their surroundings.

At the present day a surviving example, Bromley Cross, has an attraction equal to any small country station in this age of British Rail.

It is also interesting to record that the significance of this route was maintained throughout the years of British Railways ownership by the operation of a Colne–London service. The obscurity of a small Lancashire cotton town linked with the capital is more easily rationalised when one realises that Colne was an important converging point with the Midland's Skipton trains. There were three workings in each direction, excluding Sundays, this unique direct route to London ended on the 8th September, 1962.

Whilst the Manchester to Glasgow trains are remembered as a regular feature of Bolton station it is not so easily recalled that there was once a working that ran through Manchester via Miles Platting to Stockport where carriages were connected to a London bound train.

The diesel service between Bolton and Blackburn began in 1961.

3. Trinity Street, 21st August 1907. An Aspinall 'Atlantic' 4-4-2 stands alongside platform 3 with the 14.45 Manchester to Blackpool train. These locomotives at the time were the pride of the Lancashire and Yorkshire Railway, this particular engine being part of the second batch built with Hoy innovations, one of which included the cutting away of the buffer beam corners to provide more clearance through platforms. The vehicle behind the tender is a 4 wheel 'Birdcage'.

Photo: National Railway Museum

Bolton – Trinity Street

Like the Bolton & Leigh, the Bolton & Manchester station began its life as a terminus, although the similarity soon ended with the opening of the line to Preston which was accommodated with through lines on an angle to the new station. Part of the Act for the Preston line included a roadbridge over the line which was completed in 1840, in effect – Trinity Street. Another bridge had to be built for the continuation of Bridgeman Street.

With the introduction of traffic on lines to Rochdale and Blackburn, bearing in mind that at the time this was the LYR's main route to Liverpool, the original station proved totally inadequate. Enlargements took place in 1848 but the most drastic changes occurred in the late 1870's. The new work included closure and removal of Bridgeman Street, compensated somewhat by widening Trinity Street and the construction of Orlando Bridge. The access from Lever Street was compensated by a footbridge.

The extension of the platforms following along the outside of the Y Junction was less than desirable as the Manchester side was much shorter than ideal and was very restrictive especially in view of Bolton's population now closing on 150,000.

On 1st June 1880, the early aspirations of the Blackburn route were realised and Hellifield was reached on the Leeds to Carlisle route of the Midland Railway. Scottish trains from Manchester to Scotland via Bolton totalled twenty-two per day as part of St Pancras–Glasgow–Edinburgh through services but by the mid 1890's the situation at Bolton was again under scrutiny.

To ease matters the LYR had opened its route to Southport from Pendleton, Crow Nest Junction, Atherton in 1888. Avoiding routes were also added at the station, namely Johnson Street Fork at West Junction (1888), and Burnden and Rose Hill junctions in the East (1881), thus providing triangles at both ends of the station. The considerable undertaking of widening from Bolton to Bullfield and Lostock Junction continued from 1896 up until 1906, allowing the quadrupling of that section.

In the case of the station itself this had to be totally resolved and the Engineer William Hunt had the task which transpired as little short of monumental. A tender was awarded to Sir Robert Neil & Sons of Manchester who all but cleared the site and began again.

An enormous tract of land from Trinity Street to Orlando Bridge on the Manchester Road side was purchased and cleared. This had included Highfield House on High Field Street and a row of houses called Newport Terrace. All of this area was made over to the goods facilities which included a new brick goods warehouse of 160 ft in length of four stories and built adjoining an earlier warehouse of 240 ft. The earlier warehouse had hydraulic lifts whilst the new one was to be fitted with electricity. Indeed, this source of power was to play a leading role in the new station which had its own generating house alongside Trinity Street roadbridge. There were three new signalboxes, with the West cabin fitted with the first frame containing a distinctive display of small fingertip levers that engaged in three positions, their movement bringing life over the acres of junction as heavy rail sections hissed and clattered like the footsteps of giant ghosts.

The two large island platforms, 1,116 ft in length, sat astride four roads as before but with three other running lines on the outside of them, two on Trinity church side and one on the power house side. The footbridge across the west junction from Newport Street to the station in the 1880 scheme was extended from Johnson Street to Trinity Street.

The crowning opus to all these works were the street level station buildings themselves, running the length of the bridge for most of its constructed length in Accrington terra-cotta faced brick with a slate roof. There were two double arches as the entrance divided by pale pink granite pillars. The focal point was a clocktower with an octagonal arrangement of eight smaller versions of the same pillars with two ridgetop cupolas.

Platform buildings were in glazed brickwork, with a brown base and an ochre course midway, including the brick arches that curved eliptically out of a cream coloured freize with plain moulded cornice and brown string courses. Glazing in the tall doorways and windows was etched with the purpose of the rooms they enclosed.

The booking offices were of canary and mahogany wood, with racks holding a million and a half tickets. All the girder work was painted light blue. In days when Bolton was very much a coal gas fuelled borough, the station must have been quite a revelation with all its electric lighting, power for signalling, electric luggage lifts and even the locomotive turntable at Crescent Road.

To give some indication of just how necessary all this work was, on 21 June 1899, when work was started, the station was servicing 196 arrivals daily with 202 departures, the first train of the day arriving at 1.06am and the last at 11.57pm, a mere hour and a quarter of tranquility before the furore of another day began.

All this building work was tendered for at a cost of £270,018, opening some three years later, in 1903, outside the contractual time limit.

No further major work was thought necessary until 1957 when it was found that the original bridge, which had served first of all as a terminus for trams and later omnibuses, was showing signs of its age. Its deterioration was compounded further with the increasing weight and speed of vehicles in the mid-twentieth century. Although a 10 mph limit was imposed, it was, as one would expect, honoured in the breach rather than the observance. In 1962 it was decided to renew the bridge completely at a cost of £265,000, the contract being awarded to J Rata & Co Ltd, work beginning on 20th May 1968. Part of the contract was to remove the old canopy, thus giving a fresh open look to the station front albeit not as protective. The new bridge was built with concrete beams in place of the old box girder sections.

Whatever arrangements were made for locomotives in the early period is not clear, for a turntable at Bolton West Junction and a building close by with rails running into it suggests that this may have been the early shed. Another shed did once exist in the trianglular junction at Burnden, but the close proximity of this would be disadvantaged in terms of development by the obvious restrictions of the site. Consequently, new plans were drawn up in 1875 for a new hipped-roof four road shed on land adjoining Crescent Road. This was greatly expanded with the developments of the late 1890's when an eleven track section was added in 1889 of the 'Northlight' roof pattern design.

A concrete coaler and ash plant were added in 1935. One interesting development at the shed was the 50ft electric turntable, with power supplied by the generator at the station. With the introduction of larger engines, a 60ft table was needed this being installed in 1940.

The depot could claim a loyalty to steam which remained there until the very end when it was closed in July 1968.

Although the railways nationally were mortally affected by the events of 1914–1918, the period to follow proved even more traumatic with the large companies themselves absorbed into even larger concerns following the grouping as four main companies in 1923. However, it was the great industrial slump of the nineteen thirties that dealt a blow in the north-west, from which few were to effectively recover. The 1923 absorption of the LYR and LNWR into the London, Midland and Scottish Railway meant that both Bolton stations came under the same ownership.

4. Trinity Street, c.1899. A fascinating study of Bolton LYR (Trinity Street) Station in the early stages of the rebuilding programme and the turn of the century. This view from the Manchester direction shows a transitional period the large warehouse building to the left being part of the old station. Each of the archways had sets of rails running into them from the main lines and reached by means of wagon turntables which have subsequently been removed. The station 'down' platform (three), is in the process of being extended over the erstwhile sites of these turntables. The warehouse was probably retained until an advanced stage of the work, being used for the storage of building material, etc. The new style of building is evident on platforms 3 and 4, a marked contrast to the older structures opposite. Behind can be seen the towers of both stations, the older of a 'Venetian' style whilst the new tower of Victorian influence is still enclosed in scaffolding.   *Photo: Bolton Local History Museum*

As the mills went on part time or closed altogether, there was a similar repressive reaction to all supporting industries. For indeed, in 1931, the town of Wigan had 35% of its working population unemployed. Sidings fell silent with unused wagons and locomotives stored with their chimneys capped with canvas. Some of them were sent to other parts of the LMS system from which they never returned.

Following the Second World War, trade picked up but was short lived and back in the doldrums in the 1950's when Bolton still had 103 cotton mills. An indication of that industry's decline can best be illustrated by comparing relevant years. By 1966, there were only 34, but in 1979 a mere 8. In terms of Bolton's economy it is fair to say that the town was fortunate in some respects, by not being exclusively a cotton based economy as was evident by the the promoters of the Bolton & Leigh. What really changed the fortunes of the railways cartage was the fact that by January 1980 the north west had some 280 miles of motorways, a section of the M61 actually severing the route of the Bolton & Leigh on its way from Manchester to Preston.

Closure of the district stations started from 1950 and continued remorselessly throughout for eighteen years to the particularly significant year of 1968 when a number of things happened at once. Steam ceased to be used for traction by British Railways and the shed at Crescent Road closed. Trinity Street road bridge was rebuilt, an operation which included demolition of the canopy. The West End Junction track layout was simplified and shortly afterwards the Johnson Street fork was removed.

In succeeding years the diamond crossovers of the junction were simplified with the 'up' freight road disappearing all the way to Lostock Junction.

Signalling that had been undertaken by Bolton Station's three boxes came under one panel box at East Junction in December 1985 and East and West Cabins were demolished in 1987 whilst a box called 'Bolton Station Down' had been dismantled in the 1960's.

In 1987 plans formulated by Greater Manchester Council and British Rail brought about a new rail/bus interchange station on Newport Street which reduced the connection with Trinity Street to little more than a bridge over the railway, the station buildings at road level being demolished. The street has been an important focus of town life where the station with its grim canopy and picturesque shadows vied for dominance with Trinity Church, and the Railway Hotel that solidly buttressed the corner of Newport Street.

An elegant foil to all this imposition was the verandah covered pavement that sheltered waiting tramcar and later bus passengers as they circulated and used the tiny cigarette kiosk or the cosy smoky tea cabin. It was a place that bustled with a sense of movement and laughing chatter which heightened to a voluminous pitch at the beginning of the annual 'Wakes Week' holidays. All in marked contrast now an age ago, where nothing is left but a strip or tarmac and concrete enclosed by featureless bridge parapets as vehicles rush by on just another piece of road.

5. Bolton West Junction, 16th August 1914. Twenty minutes past four o'clock in the afternoon, job complete, and the tracks have been handed back by the engineer after possession. The activity seen in plates 25 and 26 has subsided and the railway can now revert to the running of its trains again. The reballasting of the tracks in the station area looks to be complete, men in the 'four' and 'six' foot tidying up and running an eye over the day's work. Compare this view with that of plate 15 when through running to and from the inside platform and through lines was still possible. Of particular note are the electric lights on their high posts, in contrast to the gas lamps along Trinity Street bridge, a feature which was the norm for the rest of the town. Overall a peaceful scene considering the First World War had broken out a few days earlier.

Photo: National Railway Museum

6. Trinity Street, c.1880. This view towards Manchester shows the station as it was during the period 1878 to 1887. Although less practical than its successor, it was certainly more pleasing from an architectural point of view. The 'venetian' tower and buildings are fronted by a graceful glazed canopy of the ridge and furrow type, a more slender version than the traditional type seen nearer the bridge. The brick built signal box, Blackburn Junction, is to a design by Smith and Yardley, the clean lines of the brickwork suggesting that the photograph was taken not long after construction, c.1876–78. A new signal box with 64 levers, was provided by the Railway Signal Company in 1888, lasting but 15 years until the remodelling of the station and introduction of electro-pneumatic system made it redundant.   *Photo: LYRS collection*

7. Trinity Street, c.1905. The new station in Trinity Street shortly after its completion in 1904. Workmen are still putting the finishing touches to the entrance canopy, a feature which perhaps hid one of the stations more attractive features. The view shows a sparsely populated street, a far cry from the present day, when a carrier could pause for a photograph in the middle of the cobbled road. We also see our first view of the tramway, the electric version which served the town for almost fifty years until abandonment in 1947.

Photo: Heyday Publishing Co Ltd

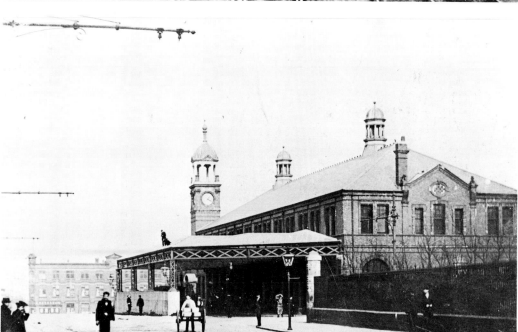

8. Trinity Street, c.1910. Hansome cabs and a horse omnibus await trade from homecoming businessmen as the evening shadows lengthen. Cobbles and tram lines recall the time of another Bolton when Trinity Street was a circulating area of people and objects on the move continuously.

Photo: Bolton Reference Library

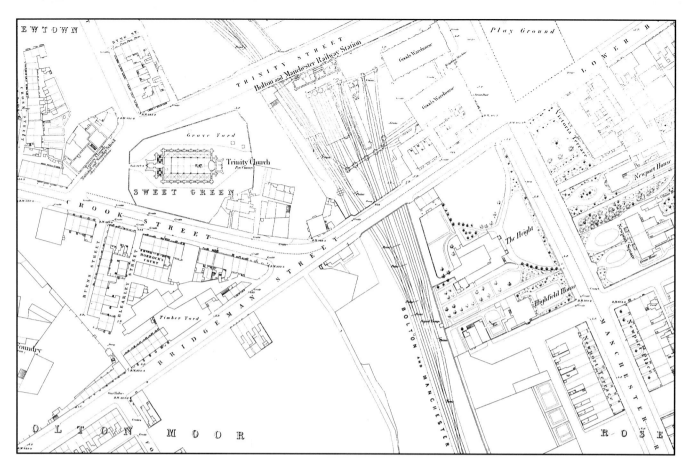

The original station of the Bolton & Manchester Railway at Trinity Street with only the Preston/Liverpool route joining it which would suggest the date of the map as being between 1839 and 1848, this latter date being when the line to Blackburn opened. Trinity Street Church serves as a constant reference point to an area that can bear little comparison to subsequent developments.

9. Trinity Street, c.1902. A photograph that produced a very unique record of the station at the time of its reconstruction. It can be seen that the platform to the right follows the tracks past Byng Street and almost to Bradshawgate tunnel. The main station buildings can also be seen to the right above the bridge parapet. Although not apparent, a poster board in the shadow of the structures indicates 'Way out over the bridge only', tending to suggest that alterations for the new station are in hand. To the right of the group on the platform are the compound stanchions which ultimately supported the girder carrying the new station building on Trinity Street. Beneath the bridge can be seen the lattice framework of Johnson Street footbridge. *Photo: Bolton Central Library*

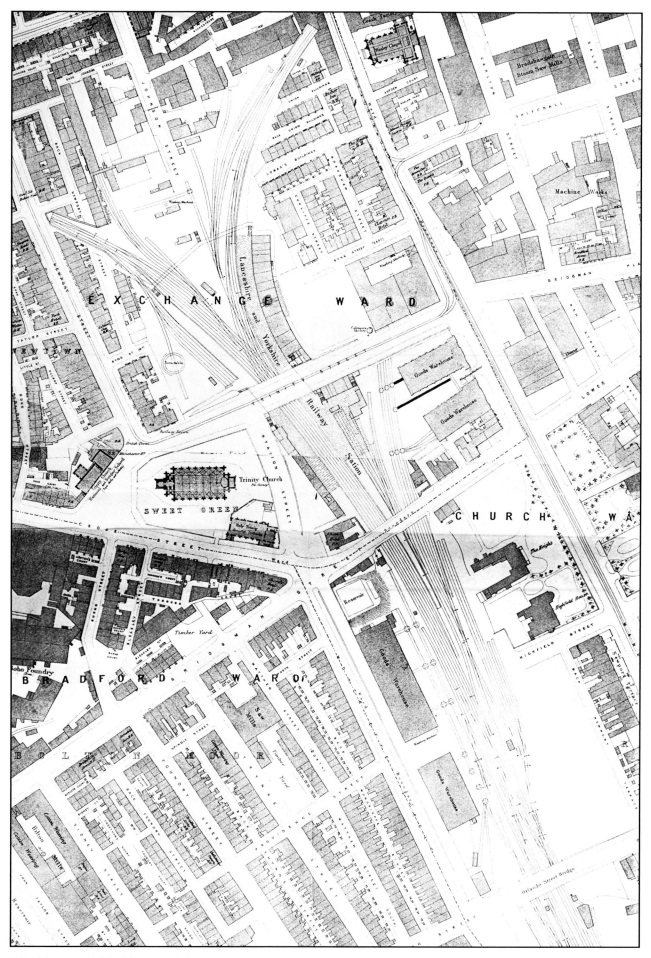

Bolton 1882. This map, published by the Bolton Corporation, shows the Lancashire and Yorkshire Railway Station adjacent to Trinity Street bridge. Note that the main buildings are on the Blackburn curve fronting Byng Street. Comparison should be made with the photograph opposite which shows the station in its transitional stage.

10. Trinity Street, 3rd December 1965. Standing alongside platform 2 with a Rochdale bound stopping train from Liverpool Exchange is a member of the much cherished 'Black' 5 Class, No. 45424, at the time an Agecroft engine. The locomotive, fitted with AWS equipment, had been a Manchester based engine for many years, previously having worked out of Patricroft shed until 1963. The three year spell at Agecroft that ensued was followed by a transfer to Springs Branch, Wigan, for the final two years of her life. One of a batch of 131 engines built in 1937 by Armstrong Whitworth, she was withdrawn in April 1968 and put in store at Carnforth prior to scrapping. This view from the Manchester end of the station shows the numerous parcels trolleys, a familiar feature at Bolton made possible by the close relationship with various mail order companies in the town. *Photo: P.E. Baughan*

11. Trinity Street, c.1955. The sheer ebullience of 'Wakes Week' not to be missed as another Class 5 locomotive, No. 45375, runs alongside platform 3 with a train forming a special for Blackpool. Scenes such as this were commonplace for the period and an example of the daily flow of passengers in 1952 showed that no less than 5,700 used some 166 trains between the hours of 5am and 9pm. These special trains were a seasonal operating feature of the area, stock being stored in siding accommodation temporarily provided at Kearsley and Moses Gate. Demands on train crews were also extensive, and a special 'link', 514 turn, was created to provide the additional manpower. Passed fireman and cleaners became drivers and firemen respectively for the duties, reverting to their normal grades at the end of each season.
Photo: Bolton Evening News

12. Trinity Street, 1939. Like a scene from a Graham Green novel with splodges of weak lighting and watery reflections. Poignantly, the clock fingers reach noon on what is apparently the end of the year as two posters proclaim 'A Happy New Year – for a Square Deal', referring to a campaign launched by the railway companies to be relieved of statutory controls imposed during the days of transport monopoly which restricted their charges whilst road competition was free to compete. The new year of 1939, hoping to be happy, was anything but, with the outbreak of war with Germany and the railways having to mark time to the inevitable conclusion of 1948. In the meantime one can reflect on matters less demanding as another poster confidently claims the virtues of a Bulldog Cigar.
Photo: Bolton Evening News

13. Trinity Street, c.1953. The Halliwell 'Pilot', is seen here making a brisk return to the shed after a turn on the Astley Bridges branch. No. 51513, one of a once numerous class, was rebuilt as a saddle tank to a design by Aspinall in 1891, but had in fact originally started life as a tender engine in 1877 to a design by Barton Wright. The locomotive is vacuum fitted for testing the vans as they came out of the warehouse. The train crew for the Halliwell 'pilot' signed on at 4.28 in the morning to be off the shed at 5.43, picking up the guard at Orlando bridge before continuing to Bullfield. Shunting duties completed, whatever there was to transfer was taken off Bullfield at 6.20am, fifteen minutes being allowed for the journey to Halliwell, frequently with a load of coal. If there was a lot of shunting at Astley Bridge and Halliwell, the engine would stay, relieving crews would arrive by tram, or in later days, bus. On its way back into Bolton, the engine would carry out any shunting required at Bradshawgate. Alternatively, she would, as on this occasion, come galloping back in the early afternoon. The old coach body in the background was used by cleaners working in the carriage sidings adjacent to Byng Street.

Photo: J. Davenport

14. Trinity Street, c.1932. An Aspinall designed 0-8-0 coal engine passes West Junction with a passenger train comprising arc roof carriages of the type attributed to a design of Mr F. Attock, L&Y Carriage and Wagon Superintendent. Interestingly, the vehicle behind the locomotive tender appears to be in Lancashire & Yorkshire livery, somewhat late but certainly not unusual. It is difficult to establish if the remaining carriages have been re-painted by the LMS but the addition of large figure three numerals on the compartment doors suggest they may have been. Apart from the smokebox number and shed plates, the scene is typically pre-group, although it is perhaps unusual to find such a type of locomotive at the head of a passenger train, particularly as it is taking the up through line. Note the pipework, between the lines, which carried air for the electro-pneumatic signalling system.

Photo: courtesy W.G. Rear

15. Bolton West Junction, 28th April 1968. A view from Johnson Street footbridge prior to the layout being simplified. To the extreme left of the picture is the power house where, in 1903, the generator commenced the supply of electricity to the new station at a time when the rest of the town was lit by coal gas, therefore becoming something of a local innovation. A vintage lower quadrant signal post dominates the foreground whilst a selection of LMS types stand alongside. The awning to the front of the station was removed between the 20th and 24th May.   *Photo: John Marshall*

16. Trinity Street, 1962. A splendid sunlit view of the western end of platform 3 – platform 4 can just be seen to the extreme right – with a 'Derby Lightweight' twin unit with Blue Square coupling code awaiting departure for the Fylde Coast. These units were in the original Brunswick Green livery with cream lining, and sported the 'speed whiskers', a feature added shortly after introduction to provide a signal warning of the vehicles' approach to people working on the track, and at level crossings. Introduced in 1958, the design later became Class 108 with many examples continuing to provide sterling service over thirty years later. To the right, elevated above the platform, is the popular tea cabin. The route indicator with code B5, was displayed for trains working the Up services between Rochdale and Blackpool North (Blackpool Central) Fleetwood via Bury. Judging by the long shadows, the service could be the 7.34pm ex-Rochdale to Blackpool North which departed Bolton at 8.4pm. The only other train to carry the B5 code was the 5.45pm ex-Rochdale to Blackpool South via Lytham, leaving Bolton at 6.17pm.   *Photo: G.H. Platt*

17. Trinity Street, c.1955. At the time this photograph was taken, British Railways Standard Class 6 locomotive No. 72003, *Clan Fraser*, was relatively new, one of ten engines designed at Derby by R.A. Riddles for either passenger or fast freight workings. Built at Crewe in 1952 for the Scottish Region, the ten engines were initially allocated equally between Polmadie (Glasgow), and Carlisle (Kingmoor). They became familiar on the Manchester–Glasgow services and in this view, with safety valves blowing, *Clan Fraser* appears eager to be away with the 9.30am ex-Manchester Victoria to Glasgow train. The 'Clans' were not a success, criticised for lack of power. The last of the class was withdrawn in 1966. No. 72003 actually lasted only ten years. However, as a schoolboy standing on the footbridge and watching one of them glide to a halt with two safety valves roaring, engulfing the lattice work in blinding white steam, it took some convincing.
Photo: Bolton Evening News

18. Bolton West Junction, c.1962. Clattering over the West Junction points, Jubilee Class No. 45584 *North West Frontier* heads a Manchester bound train into platform two with a working from Blackpool. This was a Blackpool (24E) based engine and well regarded by locomen. It was a familiar engine on the lines to Manchester and Crewe, the latter frequently with Euston expresses. To the right of the engine we see the signals on the Johnson Street avoiding line – sometimes known as the Bolton Loop – guarding the Bradshawgate and Craddock Lane section.
Photo: G.H. Platt

19. Bolton Trinity Street, 27th June 1958. Following overhaul at Horwich, Midland railway built 4F 0-6-0 No. 44019 (Wakefield-56A) runs along the Up through line with its short train, across Bolton before returning to ballast train work. Originally based at Bullfield, the ballast train was transferred to Bradshawgate Sidings where it became a firm favourite with crews on night banking duty, who, being required to wait for long periods for the next working up to Entwistle, utilized the brake van as an impromptu mess room and sleeping accommodation. *Photo: R. Keeley*

20. Bolton Trinity Street, 27th June 1958. Again on the through road, but checked at the signals, is another vintage piece of machinery, this time in the form of a Lancashire and Yorkshire Railway built 0-6-0 goods engine No. 52360, carrying out its duties as the 'Halliwell Pilot'. She is likely to be working the trip from Bullfield to the yards at Bolton East. The crew for this turn will have signed at 9.10am before taking the engine light from the shed to Bullfield to enable both sidings at East and West to be shunted. Based on an Aspinall design, the first engines of this class were introduced in 1889. The example shown here however did not appear until 1911 and was subsequently rebuilt with Belpaire firebox and extended smokebox.

No. 52360 had come to Bolton from Newton Heath and worked out its days as a grimy little 'maid of all work', mainly on shunting and trip working from one yard to another. It was withdrawn in November 1958.

Photo: R. Keeley

21. Bolton Trinity Street, 3rd April 1959. Station pilot, engine No. 50850, briefly obscures Wigan engine No. 42644 at the head of a train of stock forming what will be the 1.15pm to Liverpool Exchange (arr. 2.24). The gantry above the engine carried the walkway to the Down signal box, a somewhat precariously placed structure adjacent to platform 4. Above the retaining wall parapet is Moncrieffe Street, the houses of which were given the *coup-de-grace* as a result of railway activity and described by Malcolm Frost in the section, at the rear of the book, on Bolton Enginemen. Note also the prominent 'Billy' can, perched on the side tank of the 2-4-2 engine, a feature with a tradition not easily relinquished to the vacuum flask! *Photo: R. Keeley*

22. Trinity Street, c.1935. An excellent pictorial example of the Lancashire and Yorkshire railway designed Rail Motor alongside platform 2 *en route* from Bolton to Radcliffe. This service was introduced in 1920 and gave a sequence of operation which basically remained unchanged until withdrawal in September 1953. The 'Motor Train' as the working timetable described it, did the lion's share, but was supplemented by trains of ordinary coaching stock, the occasional working coming through from Horwich. By the late 1940s there were a dozen or so trains each way, with refinements for Saturday operation. Approximately half the trains commenced and terminated their journeys in the Bay platform at Bolton. This particular vehicle, No. 10617, was the last of a class of nine to remain in service, pottering on until March 1948.

Photo: A.G. Ellis collection

23. Bolton Trinity Street, 24th September 1965. A topographical view taken from the Manchester end of platform 2 showing the station, concrete lamp standards apart, very much as it had been since its rebuilding around the turn of the century. The following year, 1966, was to see the beginning of alterations and removals which were to change the pattern of operation for ever. The remodelling of the down side between West and Burnden Junctions was radical to say the least. The Down signal box closed on the 4th September 1966, resulting in the down passenger loop becoming a siding. The down goods loop, together with all the sidings connected to it, were to be taken out of use pending removal. Connections between the passenger loop, goods loop and sidings were to be secured in the normal position pending removal. At the west, or Preston, end of the down platform, connections between the lines previously mentioned, and the fast and slow lines i.e. the lines adjacent to platform 3 – were to be secured out of use, thus truncating and making a siding out of platform 4. In short, the whole of the west side was altered to accommodate the extensive postal and mail order business that existed, enabling road traffic direct access to the area adjacent to what had been platform 4. A minor victim of these purges was Orlando Street Ground Frame. Matters remained comparatively unchanged until March 1969 when further rationalization took away the use of the Up through line – third from left in this view – between East Junction and West Junction, meaning that all Down trains had to pass alongside platform three. Alterations affecting West Junction are dealt with later in the book.

Photo: P.E. Baughan

24. Bolton Trinity Street, 21st October 1961. Once again, an almost unchanged view of the station from the Manchester end, this time from an elevated position on Orlando Street bridge. On this occasion, a Blackpool to Manchester train, with Fleetwood portion – note fish van behind the engine – starts from platform 2, with Stanier Jubilee Class 4-6-0 No. 45679 *Armada*, with Fowler tender. The engine standing alongside on the Up through line is LMS built 4F 0-6-0 No. 44363, a Crewe Works based engine at the time, probably running in after a visit to Horwich Works. The Blackpool train over the years suffered the minor vagaries of timetable planning. Taking the LMS Working Timetable for Passenger Trains, October 6th 1947, until further notice, as an example, a train was due to leave Fleetwood at 10.15, calling at Wyre Dock some four minutes later to attach 'a wagon of fish'. Calling also at Burn Naze and Thornton for Cleveleys, it was due in Poulton at 10.41 (26 minutes for a journey normally taking twelve) to be combined with the 10.40 ex-Blackpool North to Manchester Victoria express. By 1963, British Railways had decided that the romance of steam was not for them and relegated the operation (without fish van) to a DMU, leaving Fleetwood at 10.30am to combine with the 10.45 ex-Blackpool North to Manchester Victoria. *Photo: John Marshall*

25. Bolton Trinity Street, 16th August 1914. Track renewal in earnest in the summer months of 1914 when manpower was fully utilized. The reinstatement of track alongside platform 3 nears completion but it is arguable whether or not the job is being done with new materials. Fresh ballast of any description, ash or stone, was not in evidence within the station limits although inspection of the view shown in plate 5 shows a degree of tidying up. Students of the Lancashire and Yorkshire Railway are well served by this picture. The suspended signing of station facilities shows clearly the style of lettering and board construction which was utilized by all departments. All items were detailed in a 1912 catalogue of Standard Signal Fittings issued by the company's Chief Mechanical Engineers Office, Horwich. For example, signal nameboards were given a reference S.60, and cast iron lettering U.8. Of special interest are the electro-pneumatically operated signals, the down main platform starters – above name board – having their destinations indicated on the signal arm, those visible reading from left 'Blackburn', 'Preston' and 'Blackburn'. *Photo: National Railway Museum*

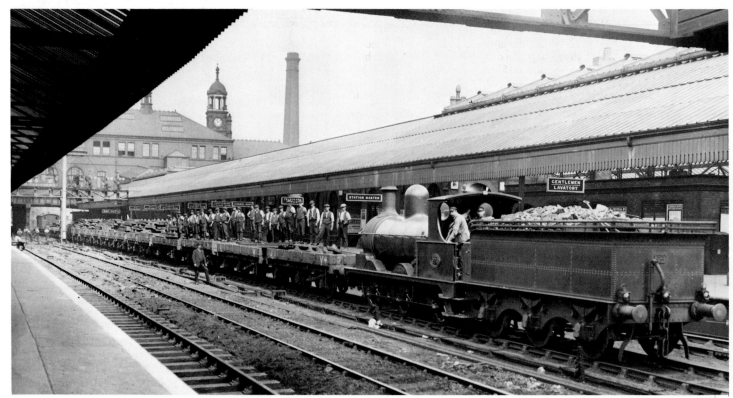

26. Bolton Trinity Street, 16th August 1914. Judging by the station clock, this scene is likely to be 11.10am on a Sunday morning with the engineer appearing to have full possession of the inner platform and through roads. The engine is a Barton Wright design, built by Beyer, Peacock in December 1887, and withdrawn in the same month 1930. *Photo: National Railway Museum*

27. Bolton Trinity Street, 8th July 1913. During their tour of Lancashire, King George V and his wife Queen Mary visited Bolton. The couple are here seen making their way down the stairs to platform 3 where the Royal Train awaits. With His Majesty is Mr John Aspinall, General Manager of the Lancashire & Yorkshire Railway Company. The Queen is accompanied by Mr Arthur Watson, then Superintendent of the line. The railway itenerary was prepared by members of the drawing office staff at Horwich and Mr Aspinall was later asked by the Royal visitors to congratulate them for their work in organising the visit.

Photo: National Railway Museum

28. Lostock, 8th July 1913. The LNWR 'Royal Train', carrying King George V and Queen Mary away from Bolton, takes the Liverpool line beyond Lostock Junction, at the site, incidentally, of an early and short lived station by the name of Chew Moor. The gleaming engine, and pride of the Lancashire & Yorkshire Railway, is a Hughes 4-6-0 No. 1514. A captivating scene as it includes a group of local people eager to share this history making visit. On a more mundane note, it is perhaps worth mentioning the track, or permanent way, still with rails 30 feet in length on an ash ballasted formation with sleeper ends protruding. This was typical L&Y practice, albeit towards the end of this method of operation.

Photo: National Railway Museum

29. (Top) Bolton Trinity Street, 7th March 1962. A series of photographs was taken by British Railways in 1962 although there does not appear to be any particular reason for the survey. This view shows the western side of the canopy that fronted the station, with Station Street to the right. Protection from the weather was welcomed by all although its presence somewhat detracted from the overall impressiveness of the red bricked building. From Trinity Street, the front elevation presented an unbalanced view, but from the front – see plate 5 – it was a perfectly symmetrical design.

30. (Lower) Bolton Trinity Street, 7th March 1962. Moving a few yards along Trinity Street we view the station front from the Manchester Road end of the town. The parking of cars and vans has not yet reached levels where it can be considered inconvenient. The canopy was to provide coverage for another six years before being removed in May 1968 in readiness for the reconstruction of Trinity Street road bridge.

31. (Above) Bolton Trinity Street, 7th March 1962. Station Street actually carried the roadway directly over the Down goods and passenger loop lines. An interesting combination was further enhanced with the presence of tram lines – note the two 'smooth' lines to the left of the bus – which served routes 'G' and 'M' to and from Great Lever and Swan Lane respectively. *Photo: British Rail*

32. (Centre) Bolton Trinity Street, 7th March 1962. From the western corner of Station Street's junction with Trinity Street, we look over the hump of the bridge that was to be replaced in 1968. Until construction of a purpose built bus station, Trinity Street was one of several locations which served as terminus for the Corporation's extensive bus system, in fact it was to take several years before the rail and bus services were re-integrated with the building of a new rail station at the corner of Newport Street. *Photo: British Rail*

33. Bolton Trinity Street, 7th March 1962. The impressive clock tower can now be appreciated as the photographer withdraws down Trinity Street to take a wider angle view. Motor car enthusiasts are adequately catered for – how prophetic that the Ford Anglia and Jaguar cars face one another. Long gone are the days when the *Daily Telegraph* would be purchased for five pence (2½p) and one could escape to Blackpool, and return, for 5/6 (27½p). *Photo: British Rail*

34. Bolton Trinity Street, 7th March 1962. Compare this view with that in plate 12. Some three decades separate them but change has been minimal. The stairway to platforms 1 and 2 is at the far end on the right. West and northbound passengers keep to the right of W.H. Smith. *Photo: British Rail*

35. Bolton Trinity Street, 7th March 1962. The ticket windows to the left remind us of busier days, or perhaps of hopes that did not materialize. The effects of Beeching were still to be felt and apart from the odd closure i.e. Turton (cl. 6.2.61), The Oaks (cl. 6.11.50), Darcy Lever (cl. 29.10.51) and Dixon Fold (cl. 18.5.31), the areas served via the former L&Y lines around Bolton still retained their passenger trains. *Photo: British Rail*

36. Bolton Trinity Street, 7th March 1962. Whatever the time of day – both clocks are different – the photographer does not appear to be taking his life in his hands, even if one of Magee's lorries is bearing down. Wednesdays cannot always have been as quiet as this but here is the evidence. The station will no doubt be prepared for the Easter weekend when full and half day excursions to Blackpool, Southport, Morecambe were the norm. There would also be dozens of excursions from all over the north of England passing through to a variety of destinations. Easter Sunday for instance, witnessed the passage of some rare examples – Mossley to Liverpool, Coventry to Colne, to name but two. *Photo: British Rail*

37. Trinity Street, 7th March 1962. A view and location familiar to generations of Boltonians. The entrance to Johnson Street footbridge, which provided a short cut from the town centre as well as a haven for trainspotters. It also appears difficult to take pictures of Bolton without including the town hall, again raising itself above the glazed canopy. The bus serving route No. 35 – Horwich via Chorley New Road – used Trinity Street as its town terminus.

38. (Centre) Trinity Street, c.1933. Electric trains through Bolton! One may well ask, although the procedure was not unusual as this view at West Junction illustrates. A train of MSJ&A – Manchester South Junction and Altrincham – stock is being taken along the down through line to Horwich Works for overhaul. However, the signals show that it is to transfer to the slow line between here and Lostock Junction. Note the erstwhile canopy which extended along the faces of platforms three and four, the remains of which were finally removed when Trinity Street bridge was reconstructed.

Photo: courtesy W.G. Rear

39. (Lower) Trinity Street, 7th March 1962. Although nearly three decades separate this view with the one above, only vegetation has changed to any large extent. The signalling has retained its antiquity and to the right are the erstwhile Byng Street carriage sidings where stock was serviced. In this view the lone occupant is one of Cravens Diesel Multiple Units, distinguished by the two large windows in the front end. Johnson Street footbridge, seen in numerous other illustrations in the book, was a focal point of the station for some eight decades. The four spans at the town end were wrought iron, dating from 1887. With the reconstruction of the station in 1899, the bridge was extended by three spans to Trinity Street to take the form seen here. This new structure was made of steel with a concrete decking. It became bridge number 5 on the Bolton to Euxton Junction line and was completely removed in July 1981.

40. Bolton – Manchester Road, 15th January 1932. Although the reconstruction of Trinity Street Station was more in the public eye, one could not be less than impressed by the massive goods warehouse that appeared on the east side of the line parallel with Manchester Road. The brick structure was termed as an 'extension' to the 1885 building but in essence, literally dwarfed it. Completed in 1904 as a contemporary of the station, it had features typical of Lancashire and Yorkshire civil engineering practice. The identity along the side walls of the London Midland and Scottish railway came about following a fire which badly damaged the building in September 1918. Obviously taking several years to complete the refurbishment, this view shows the Orlando Street end with equipment of its new owners in evidence, even the motive power has been put in the hands of the 'enemy' in the form of an ex-LNWR locomotive. The fire ravaged area was concentrated around the centre of the building – note the 'new' section in the centre. *Photo: National Railway Museum*

41. Bolton Trinity Street, 20th August 1963. Drifting along the down through 'road' with a fully laden mineral wagon train is LMS built 2-6-0 No. 42727, an Aintree based engine. Built originally as class 4, it was ultimately classified as 6P5F, illustrating its usefulness as a mixed traffic engine. This particular locomotive was built at Horwich in 1927 to a Hughes design under Fowlers direction. Out of a total of 245 engines, No. 42727 was one of the last pair to survive, being withdrawn in 1967. The signals in the right background controlled the lines at Bolton East Junction where the route to Castleton and Rochdale left the Manchester lines. Orlando Street bridge crosses the railway to the rear of the train. It was necessary to extend the bridge some 170 feet in an easterly direction in 1901 to accommodate the new extensions to the goods yard along Manchester Road. *Photo: B.K.B. Green*

42. (Above) Bolton East Junction, 26th July 1963. Threading its way past East Junction signal box to gain the platform road is Stanier 2-cylinder 2-6-4T No. 42652 with what is thought to be the 4.43pm ex-Manchester Victoria to Horwich train. Bolton East signal box, located between the fast lines, was a brick built structure dating from 1902. It had a 145 lever frame and was the largest of the Bolton signalling installations. It was closed on the 8th December 1985, along with Burnden Junction box, although its use had diminished as a result of the September 1966 remodelling, reducing its number of working levers to 95. *Photo: P. Reeves*

43. Bolton East Junction, 26th July 1963. A somewhat grimy Class 5, No. 45227, passes the signal box on its last lap of the journey with the 3.20pm Blackpool South to Manchester Victoria train. This particular working called at Blackpool South, Squire's Gate, St. Annes, Ansdell, Lytham and Kirkham before a thirteen minute sprint for the 8 mile run to Preston. Stops at Leyland and Chorley preceded a thirteen minute call at Bolton, the train leaving at 5.3pm. On Saturdays, the journey time was two minutes longer.

Photo: P. Reeves

44. Bolton East, 26th July 1963. Having rounded the curve from the Castleton line, Stanier Class 5 No. 45078 crosses over to the slow lines on the approach to Trinity Street. The train is the 4.35pm Rochdale to Blackpool Central, which, during the week (Saturday Excepted), called at Castleton, Heywood and Bury Knowsley Street on its way to Bolton. Departure at 5.6pm allowed for a call at Chorley before running express to Kirkham where the train stopped to set down only, similarly for the stations via Lytham to Blackpool Central. The lightweight lattice structure beyond the signal box is Lever Street footbridge, erected in 1902 in line with the then remodelling of the station.

Photo: P. Reeves

45. Bolton East Junction, 26th July 1963. Another from Lever Street footbridge, this time looking east, as another Stanier Class 5, No. 45375, comes off the Castleton line with 4.25pm Rochdale to Southport train. Having called at all stations via Bury Knowsley Street, the train will leave Bolton at 5 o'clock, calling at Lostock Junction and Westhoughton to pick up only, Hindley North and Wigan Wallgate, before running non stop to Southport initially at St. Lukes, and then Chapel Street. The businessman from Manchester was provided with a connecting express service which left Victoria at 4.40pm.
Photo: P. Reeves

46. Bolton East Junction, 19th April 1968. Mundane duties indeed for one of Staniers 8F locomotives No. 48773 as she shunts vans on 'B' side in the Arrival siding adjacent to the Castleton line between East Junction and Rose Hill Junction. The bridge girders in the background carried the railway over Manchester Road, not very far away from Burnden Park, home of the town football team – note the floodlight pylons. The engine had been at Bolton for three years and was shortly to be transferred to Rose Grove prior to withdrawal. Life however carried on for No. 48773 and she survived to be preserved on the Severn Valley Railway.
Photo: N.R. Knight

47. Bolton East Junction, 26th July 1963. A view from the footbridge at Lever Street over East Junction sees LMS built 'Crab' 2-6-0 No. 42725, a Bolton engine, hauling a mixture of loaded wagons out of 'Haslams' sidings on to the Down Goods line, with a trip working to Halliwell Goods. It is thought that this particular working was to take the residue of traffic after the booked trips had completed their turns. To the left of the picture are sidings on the 'B' side, whilst those to the extreme right served the 'A' side.
Photo: P. Reeves

48. (Above) Bolton MPD, 3rd August 1936. Against the backdrop of Beehive Spinning Company's Mill, with which the Bolton steam shed became visually identified, this view of the near empty building illustrates a typical Bank Holiday when, quite literally, anything that moved was put into traffic. The intensity of Bolton's suburban passenger services and goods movements assured that a Bolton shedplate was no sinecure for either locomotives or enginemen. The original shed on the site, that to the left with the pitched roof, had four roads and opened in 1875. The extension was added in 1889. This view, taken from the coaling plant, illustrates the shed after improvements had been made by the LMS. The previous year the C14 code that the shed had retained since its Lancashire and Yorkshire days was changed to 26C, an identity well known and revered until September 1963. It finally adopted 9K as its code, this lasting until closure of the depot from 30th June 1968.   *Photo: A.G. Ellis collection*

49. Bolton MPD, 12th May 1935. One time pride of the LNWR, at rest on the former L&Y shed, is a 'Prince of Wales' class 4P 4-6-0 No. 25797, a design introduced in 1911. Four engines of the class came to Bolton in the mid nineteen thirties to work a superannuated life on local suburban services. Note the original hipped roof shed of the 1870s behind the engine. Both this and the extension to the right were re-roofed later with a concrete louvre type structure (see plate 59).   *Photo A.G. Ellis collection*

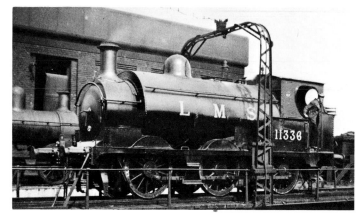

50. Bolton MPD, c.1937. A well turned out saddle tank on the electric turntable at the Crescent Road shed. These Class 2F engines were originally introduced in 1877 with tenders to a design by Barton Wright. Conversion to 0-6-0 Saddle Tanks came about as a result of an 1891 modification by Aspinall. No. 11336 became British Railways 51336 and finished its working life at Fleetwood in 1960 after many years of association with Newton Heath. This visit to Bolton was probably after being outshopped from Horwich, to which it was ultimately taken in late 1960 for scrapping. The turntable was an innovation of Bolton shed, which had been equipped with electric power as early as 1903!
Photo: LGRP courtesy David & Charles

51. Bolton MPD, 1947. Getting towards the end of its life, this former Lancashire and Yorkshire built 0-8-0 rests on shed between duties. A total of eighteen of these Class 7F locomotives were taken into British Railways stock, a small number of survivors going on to be renumbered with a 5 replacing the 1.   *Photo: N.R. Knight*

52. Bolton, 9th August 1953. A member of the once numerous 2-4-2 side tank engines of the Bolton allocation. They typified the motive power requirements of the L&Y for short intensive suburban working and nearly every depot had members of the class. Outwardly, No. 50731 looks to be in better condition than those in the view below, but it was to be withdrawn some two years after this view following a superannuated spell on station pilot duties. *Photo: A.G. Ellis collection*

53. Bolton, c.1960. We take a final look at former 'Lanky' engines with this view of an unrebuilt member of the Aspinall designed goods engines. After a lengthy spell at Crewe Works, No. 52345 came to Bolton in 1959 to spend its last three years of activity. It was withdrawn in September 1962 and stored out of use at the shed for several months before being scrapped in May 1963. *Photo: Author's collection*

54. Bolton MPD, 27th November 1955. Engines stored out of use in the shed siding, and, perhaps not surprisingly, all of Lancashire and Yorkshire Railway vintage. The 2-4-2T in the foreground, No. 50850, was one of a number rebuilt in 1898 with longer tanks and a 4 tons coal capacity. It was transferred to Southport (27C) in February 1960 and was finally withdrawn in the autumn of 1961 prior to being scrapped at Crewe Works. Other modifications had included a 1910 rebuild with Belpaire firebox and extended smokebox. Second from left, the Aspinall 0-6-0 Class 3F tender engine No. 52139, survived to the end of 1960 after a four year spell at Mirfield. It was taken to Horwich for scrapping at the end of that year. The third engine, another 2-4-2T, No. 50655, had been a Rose Grove (24B) allocation and was a member of the class rebuilt to a design of 1910 which included fitting of a Belpaire boiler. The other 0-6-0 tender engine to the right of the picture, No. 52431, was subsequently transferred to Lower Darwen for a short spell before ending its working days at Newton Heath. Withdrawn in November 1959, it was kept in store for over two years before being scrapped.

Photo: F.W. Shuttleworth

55. Bolton MPD, c.1955. One of three 0-8-0 Class 7F locomotives on Bolton shed in the nineteen fifties, No. 49532 was of a type designed by Fowler for the LMS and built at Crewe in 1931, two years after the class had been introduced. She was one of six of the class withdrawn in 1956. The Bolton allocation were used for heavy local colliery work, in particular those undertakings served from Kearsley Sidings. The majority of the class spent their final days concentrating on work over former Lancashire and Yorkshire lines, the last members being withdrawn from Agecroft Shed at the end of 1961. *Photo: Phil Vaughan*

56. Bolton MPD, c.1955. 'Handsome is as handsome does', a locomotive that drew superlative praise from local enginemen, along with Stanier's other masterpiece, the 'Black' Five, as being very well suited to the short suburban workings that typified Bolton's services: the engine, No. 42565 along with 42626 and 42472, was favoured with one of the prestige workings of the day, the 5.40pm ex-Manchester Victoria to Hellifield. Operated by a Bolton crew, this train, sometimes having as many as nine carriages, ran express to Bolton, arriving at 5.56. Departing two minutes later, Darwen was the next stop on the way to Blackburn (arrive 6.25). From this point, it was all stations, with the exception of Newsholme, to Hellifield and a 7.20 arrival. *Photo: Phil Vaughan*

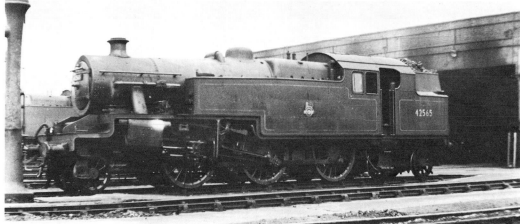

57. Bolton MPD, September 1960. These mixed traffic engines designed by Riddles were introduced in 1953. This particular engine, No. 84019, was initially allocated to Bury (26D), and apart from a short spell at Lees (26E), spent most of its life at Bolton, where its duties consisted mainly of the railmotor runs on the Horwich branch, and services to Chorley and Radcliffe. It was transferred to Stockport (9B) in December 1965 and withdrawn two months later. *Photo: Photomatic*

58. Bolton MPD, 30th July 1950. Having just been outshopped from Horwich, No. 40119, a Kentish Town (14B) locomotive, awaits a running in turn. Many engines were dealt with in this way from Bolton prior to being returned to their home depot, in fact the freight working timetable contained details of numerous movement requiring timings to and from Horwich Works. Two in particular, indicated as Trial Trips, and operated on a 'run as required' basis, were timed to leave the works at 11.20am and 1.20pm respectively. The first worked in a clockwise direction via Chorley, Cherry Tree, and Blackburn, the other in the opposite direction via Bolton. Reversal at Blackburn was necessary in either instance although on occasions however, according to foot-plateman Jim Markland, a trial trip would be curtailed say, at Adlington, if all was in order. *Photo: N.R. Knight*

59. Bolton MPD, c.1955. The Crescent Road shed at a time in the mid nineteen fifties after alterations to the buildings had been completed, notably to the roof structure. A very typical assembly of Bolton's motive power for the period, enhanced by the presence of Stanier's popular class 4 passenger tank engines and a pair of the Horwich 'Crab' 2-6-0s. Hidden away somewhat are two Stanier versions of the same wheel arrangement. The prominent locomotive, No. 42655, was at Bolton for many years until withdrawal in 1963. It was taken to Horwich works for the final act.

Photo: Bolton Evening News

60. Bolton MPD, 29th March 1965. Probably returning from its rail-motor duties at Blackrod, BR Standard Class 2 2-6-2T No. 84025 stands on the Ashpit road. The original water tank and coal 'hole' are to the right, with the mechanical ferro concrete structure that replaced it in the background.

Photo: Steve Leyland

61. Bolton MPD, 1968. A last glimpse of the depot with Stanier 8F 2-8-0 No. 48773 – now preserved on the Severn Valley Railway – waiting to go off shed. This period was to see the end of steam on Bolton shed and it is perhaps fitting that one of the last occupants should remain in harness to this day.

Photo: N.R. Knight

62. Moses Gate, 21st October 1961. The colliery owner, Mr Hulton, applied for and succeeded in getting increased facilities for loading railway wagons with coke at Moses Gate, no doubt improving the revenue of this the first station out of Bolton on the Manchester line. This view towards Bolton from the Down platform shows Stanier 2-6-4T No. 42565 arriving with a local stopping train for Manchester Victoria. Unfortunately, it does not show the extensive goods sidings that existed on both sides of the line between here and Bolton. There were four tracks for most of the way, requiring two signal boxes, Moses Gate No. 1, which closed in 1935 and No. 2, a brick structure from 1900 which lasted until 1975. *Photo: John Marshall*

63. Moses Gate, 9th June 1966. This view towards Manchester unfortunately portrays the start of the decline in many of the local railway stations. The canopies have been removed to make way for rudimentary waiting shelters although the passenger is still able to keep dry on his or her long walk down the walkways. The station still however retains that 'influence' of the Lancashire & Yorkshire Railway Booking Office building which was located over the tracks and dated from 1888 when the improvements were carried out.

Photo: P.E. Baughan

64. Moses Gate, c.1926. The district of Moses Gate was blessed with a goodly supply of public transport. During weekdays, upwards of thirty trains called in each direction for the three minute journey to/from Bolton. The area was also well served by trams as this view along Bolton Road illustrates. The letter 'F' indicates the route code, in this case for the Farnworth service, the terminus being at the Black Horse. This particular service lasted until the 12th November 1944 although trams did continue along the route as far as the Borough boundary on Saturdays (for football traffic), and Sunday mornings, until the end of the 1945/46 football season. At this point the Maroon and Cream trams of Bolton Corporation are standing on South Lancashire Transport metals, whose routes were used to reach Walkden. The lines in the left foreground connected Bolton Road with Egerton Street.

Photo: courtesy E. Gray

65. Farnworth, 28th January 1975.
On a cold winters day, the entrance to Farnworth Station in Bridge Street looks even more miserable, although the thought of a 'night out' in London at £6 – note the poster on the right – might prove something of an attraction. The station was extensively rebuilt in 1890 with increased covered accommodation at platform level, some of the roofing from Bootle being dismantled and re-erected.
Photo: Author's collection

66. Farnworth, 28th January 1975.
This view from the corner of Cemetery Road shows the building thought to have been provided for Tunnel station at Farnworth in 1838, and which became Halshaw Moor in 1845. Seven years later, another change was made this time to Halshaw Moor and Farnworth, and finally Farnworth and Halshaw Moor in 1870. It has always been purely a passenger station, without even so much as a crossover for trains. However a small Smith and Yardley signal box with six levers had existed on the down side between 1872 and 1935. *Photo: Author's collection*

67. Farnworth, 1st August 1966. In this view south towards Manchester, a Stanier Class 5MT is just leaving the 'Down' tunnel with a Bolton bound parcels train. The tunnel was built alongside the original 1838 'bore' and opened on the 5th December 1880, thus allowing the singling of the now 'Up' side tunnel. The requirement of this new tunnel was apparently to provide sufficient clearance for Midland Railway Pullman carriages which it was intended to run between Scotland and Manchester via the Settle and Carlisle line. Once again we see typical architectural features of Lancashire and Yorkshire Railway in the station structures.
Photo: G.J. Biddle

68. Kearsley, 5th June 1961. Just after five o'clock in the afternoon, one of Bolton's (26C) 2-6-4 tank engines, No. 42289, pulls away from Kearsley with the ex-4.43 Manchester Victoria to Horwich train, making light work of the 1 in 186 gradient on the climb to Farnworth Tunnel. A working to these timings had been in operation for many years, providing an all stations – Salford excepted – service to Horwich via the Fork line. *Photo: P. Reeves*

69. Kearsley, 5th June 1961. A rather grimy 'Crab' 2-6-0 No. 42710, awaits departure with the 5.18 ex-Manchester Victoria to Bolton stopping train. This Newton Heath based engine was withdrawn in 1965 after being stored at Bolton, although in its last couple of years it had paid short visits to Gorton and Stockport. *Photo: P. Reeves*

70. Kearsley, 5th June 1961. Kearsley station in late afternoon was, by today's standards, extremely busy, with a variety of trains passing through on their way to an equally variable number of destinations. One such working was the 4.3pm Manchester Victoria to Blackpool North with through carriages for Barrow-in-Furness which were detached at Preston. On this occasion Longsight 'Jubilee' 4-6-0 No. 45736 *Phoenix*, a rebuilt member of the class, makes a stirring sight as she passes through the station, the cooling towers and chimneys of the nearby power station providing a background which is now but a memory. *Phoenix* had been a Crewe engine for many years, having in fact been built there in 1936. She was rebuilt in 1942 with a larger boiler and withdrawn in 1964, a year which saw the largest single numbers of the class made redundant. The history of the train seen here is not as clear, although less than a decade earlier, Barrow had been served by a separate working from Manchester Exchange. That too was the fragmented remains of a wartime service to Glasgow, which had run via Tyldesley and Wigan North Western. *Photo: P. Reeves*

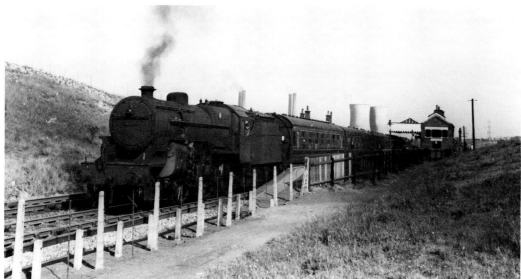

71. Kearsley, c.1910. Intermediate station on the Manchester & Bolton Railway, Kearsley first appeared as Ringley when the line opened in 1838. Shortly after, the name of Stoneclough was adopted before becoming Stoneclough & Kearsley in 1894. The singular name of Kearsley appeared in 1903 shortly after the rebuilding of the station in the form seen here. This view towards Bolton shows an array of enamel signs that provided a variety of colour to comparatively staid railway company liveries.

Photo: Heydey Publishing Company

72. Kearsley, 16th July 1965. This view towards Bolton taken from a northbound dmu shows a little changed station from that shown above. A Manchester bound Craven's dmu, distinguished by the two large windows, leaves the up platform with the 11.28am (ex-Bolton) train. The parapets to the stone arch over Stoneclough Road are in the foreground.

Photo: P.E. Baughan

73. Kearsley, 31st July 1963. This early morning view of Kearsley shows the 7.28am train to Manchester about to cross Stoneclough Road bridge. The working, due in Manchester at 7.43, commenced its journey from Colne.

Photo: P. Reeves

Kearsley Branch

Built to provide an outlet for coal from the Bridgewater Collieries, this short but steeply graded branch opened on 28th February 1878. There were actually two branches, the second, a much shorter line serving Stony Hill Colliery, opened at the same time lasted only a decade before closure of the coal workings rendered it redundant. However, the 1 mile 13 chain line described here provided a connection on Linnyshaw Moss with the Bridgewater Collieries Railway by means of exchange sidings. The branch was originally double track and commenced at Kearsley Junction where there were extensive sidings on the down side of the Bolton to Manchester line with space for 224 wagons. The three quarters of a mile climb from the sidings to Linnyshaw Moss was on a 1 in 45 gradient which levelled out on reaching the exchange point. The branch was singled in 1930, but evidence to its period of double track operation can clearly be seen in the following series of photographs.

74. Kearsley Sidings, c.1960. Waiting patiently with its short train of mineral wagons in the Exchange sidings W.D. 'Austerity' 2-8-0 No. 90725, a Bolton engine, was a regular performer on this turn. There were numerous slots during the day which allowed ten minutes for the climb to Linnyshaw Moss, either with empty wagons or trains of coal from Clifton, brought in by an Agecroft engine, which was going for washing. Jim Markland remembers occasions when as many as 40 empties were taken up frequently hauled by an 'Austin Seven', 0-8-0, freight engine. When descending with a loaded train it was necessary to pin down up to fifteen or sixteen sets of brakes. There was no telephone communication between the two points so it was not uncommon for engine and brake van to provide the link.   *Photo: N.R. Knight*

75. Kearsley Branch Sidings, c.1960. Signalling was minimal on the branch which was operated by Annetts Key. Originally, a brick built Smith and Yardley signal box containing a 12-lever frame served the lower end of the branch. Singling of the line probably brought about the box's demise although there is little evidence as to the actual date. However, it is thought that the small structure seen here, with *Kearsley* in L&Y lettering, and *Branch Sidings* in the LMS variety, dates from 1927. The frame was renewed in 1947, being brought into use on the 6th May at a site marginally further up the branch.   *Photo: N.R. Knight*

76. Kearsley Branch, c.1960. Leaving the Exchange Sidings, the train starts its climb in earnest. The line on the left, since singling in 1930 has become a head shunt, note the catch point to arrest erring vehicles.
Photo: N.R. Knight

77. Kearsley Branch, c.1960. The photographer uses the rear of the brake
continued over

77 continued

van to good advantage to capture this view back towards the junction. To the left is Stoneclough Road, seen here passing beneath the Manchester and Bolton line just south of Kearsley Station. The masonry bridge was typical of canal architecture, emphasised by the deep construction technique.

Photo: N.R. Knight

78. (Top of page) Kearsley Branch, c.1960. Still climbing, 90725 envelopes itself in steam and smoke, perhaps showing signs of ageing machinery or minimal maintenance or both. The engine remained at Bolton until September 1962 but following a brief spell at Fleetwood, finished its days at Rose Grove in August 1965.

Photo: N.R. Knight

79. (Second from top) Kearsley Branch, c.1960. This view from Bolton Road overbridge shows the branch as it crosses Roscow Road level crossing and curves west from its parallel course with Stoneclough Road. Note the width of the formation, evidence of its double track days. *Photo: N.R. Knight*

80. (Third from top) Kearsley Branch, c.1960. Having reached the summit of the line and the point past which BR engines must not go, the Foreman Shunter, who has travelled on the footplate, sets the points for the next stage of operation. At this point the colliery engine will be collecting the wagons. Linnyshaw Moss Sidings were closed to traffic on the 26th June 1966 and the connection leading to the Colliery taken away. *Photo: N.R. Knight*

81. (Below-left) Linnyshaw Moss, c.1960. Having delivered its train, 90725 prepares to return to Kearsley Junction. The location is approximately at a point now obliterated by the M61 motorway where it forms a junction with the A666 Kearsley By-Pass.

Photo: N.R. Knight

82. (Below-right) Linnyshaw Moss, c.1960. The colliery engine, an 0-6-0 Saddle Tank named *Wizard*, takes the strain of a train of wagons of a length that can be described as impressive.

Photo: N.R. Knight

Darcy Lever

At just over a mile from the town centre, Darcy Lever station was the closest of all to Bolton and as such it is remarkable that it lasted until the 29th October 1951, given the expansive development of Bolton's road transport. What may have relieved the situation to some degree was the fact that it was on a steam railmotor route from Bolton to Bradley Fold and Radcliffe. When exactly the station opened is not clear but at the time there was very little in the vicinity. Certainly it was there in 1860 when there was little else but Haulgh Hall, this may well have been the reason for its existence. Much of the land in this area was owned by the Earl of Bradford who was also involved with the local Doe Mine workings. As it developed, Darcy Lever lived very much as a separate village with unconcealed independence from the large County Borough. Probably due to its clean washing prowess, it earned the nickname 'Dolly Tub City'.

84. Darcy Lever, August 1953. 'Crab' 2-6-0 No. 42827 heads an engineering train over Darcy Lever viaduct on its way to Bolton. This wrought iron structure of eight spans was built on stone piers and abutments dating from 1848, the girders themselves being very early examples of the lattice type. Renewal of the ironwork was carried out between 1881 and 1883, with the timber decking being replaced by pre-cast concrete in 1958. Carrying the Castleton to Bolton line over the River Tonge and Radcliffe Road at a height of over 80 feet, the structure was finally designated non-operational in 1983, some thirteen years after the line closed. *Photo: F. Mills*

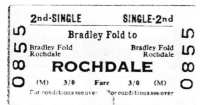

85. Bradley Fold West, c.1964. The goods loops between this point and Bradley Fold Station provided refuge and watering facilities for the slower moving freight trains, in particular those which had just come from the local colliery. This view east towards Bury shows the all timber Lancashire and Yorkshire Railway signal box which contained a 20 lever frame and was built in 1911. The box was closed and the loops taken out of use on 5th November 1967, the block section being extended from the station box to Rose Hill junction.

Photo: LYRS collection

83. Darcy Lever, c.1950/51. The first station out from Trinity Street on the Castleton line was Darcy Lever and it was the nearest of the former L&Y stations to the town centre, a fact which no doubt brought about its early demise. The rather ungainly footbridge was a wrought iron lattice girder affair supported on brick piers, the structure being No. 46 in the Castleton to Bolton Line bridge register. The view here towards Bolton shows what is possibly a Southport working on its way to Rochdale. The locomotive is one of the LMS built 3-cylinder 4-4-0 Compounds, No. 41186, which finished its working life at Lancaster Green Ayre after a lengthy spell at Southport. The platform to the right has been reconstructed using LMS pattern concrete units whilst that to the left retained its traditional timber facing and gravel surfacing. The station buildings were an attempt by the company to standardise and were fairly lightweight in their construction. The station, although closed on 29th October 1951, latterly had over twenty trains each way, mostly on the Horwich–Bolton– Radcliffe/Rochdale services. There was one working however, the 7.31a.m. to Bolton, which had left Manchester Victoria at 6.5 to run via Oldham and Rochdale. It was also possible to catch direct trains to Southport and Liverpool, albeit one or two each day. *Photo: Bolton Evening News*

86. Bradley Fold, c.1964. Bradley Fold Station signal box was of a design adopted by the Lancashire and Yorkshire railway as its standard. Originally, the structure was all timber with the nameboard on the front overlooking the running lines. There was a 32 lever frame with numbers 1 and 2 operating the gate lock and steps respectively. Rationalization of operating facilities was introduced in 1967 when, from 17th May, signal boxes at Bradley Fold East, Bradley Fold Junction and Bury Gas Works were closed to extend the block section from Bradley Fold Station to Bury Knowsley Street West. Signalling functions remaining were shared between the station box and a new ground frame adjacent to East box.

Photo: LYRS collection

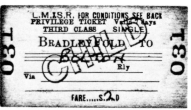

87. Bradley Fold, c.1964. View from the down platform looking west towards Bolton. Comparison should be made with the view below to see what effect a period of over fifty years had on the scene. The footbridge is now of a more modern design in concrete, having replaced the earlier structure in 1953. It has been found necessary to reconstruct the signal box base in brick and signals have become upper quadrant types on steel columns, both tubular and lattice types. Elsewhere, the changes are of a cosmetic nature i.e. signs, gas lamps etc.

Photo: LYRS collection

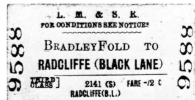

88. Bradley Fold, c.1910. An early view of the station, again looking towards Bolton. Through the footbridge (erected 1885) we can see the up and down goods loops which ended at Bradley Fold West box, 1,313 yards away. Passenger services were withdrawn from the 5th October 1970, an unfortunate decision when one considers the development that has since taken place along the route. Although basically on the Rochdale to Bolton service in its latter years, it was possible to travel direct to Liverpool Exchange, Southport, Blackpool, Wigan etc., and as late as 1963 there were 26 west and 25 eastbound trains calling. *Photo: LYRS collection*

Bolton West and the Blackburn Line

89. Bolton West. The signal box interior shortly after being brought into service. It was operated electro-pneumatically, the first installation of its kind in the country and replaced two earlier signal boxes, Blackburn Junction, a 64 lever Railway Signal Company box of 1888, and Johnson Street Fork Junction, another brick built 34 lever Railway Signal Company box, also of 1888. Commissioning took place on 27th September 1903 and the 83 lever frame had nine spares. Of particular interest in this view are the lever plates with top and bottom positions, the levers being in neutral in the centre position. The operation was less arduous than that of a mechanical box with its long pull levers, but would require constant diligence as Bolton West was a very busy junction with restricted sighting. Note the megaphone, the signal box being situated in a very open site. Rationalization in the area resulted in closure of this and Bolton East box from the 8th December 1985, the remaining signalling requirements being taken care of by a modern sectional building adjacent to Orlando Street bridge on the Up side. Early in 1990, Bolton area signalling came under Manchester Piccadilly. *Photo: National Railway Museum*

90. Johnson Street Junction, c.1955. The Johnson Street Fork or avoiding lines at the western end of Bolton Station. Even at this late date L&Y signals were in evidence, note this freshly painted example, situated on the opposite side of the tracks for sighting purposes. The signals themselves, the home (upper), guard the junction but the distants (lower) are for Bradshawgate, a signal box beyond the tunnel on the Blackburn line that was closed on 2nd June 1968. To the right, carriages are stored in Byng Street Sidings, usually for trains operating east of Bolton, particularly to Rochdale. In the centre is probably the most unremarkable of tunnel entrances, Bradshawgate. *Photo: LYRS collection*

91. (Above) & 92 (Below) Johnson Street Fork, 18th May 1968. Passenger trains over unusual lines is probably how this event would be described. A rail tour organized by the Warwickshire Railway Society traversed the Fork line during its journey between Birmingham and Carnforth. Under the heading of 'North Western Steam Tour' the train was to take a route via Wolverhampton, Stoke, Stockport, Rochdale, Todmorden, Burnley, Blackburn, Bolton, Preston and Blackpool North before reversing to complete the outward leg by way of Lostock Hall, Blackburn and Hellifield. The journey home was no less interesting, commencing with a detour to Morecambe on to Preston and Warrington before turning inland at Hartford Junction for a brief encounter with the CLC as far as Altrincham. A second visit to Stockport was followed by more conventional routeing which saw the event return to its West Midlands base via Crewe and Stafford. It was perhaps fitting that the leading locomotive, 'Stanier' Class 5 No. 44949, should be prominent as it had spent most of its latter years in the area at both Rose Grove and Newton Heath respectively. Johnson Street Fork, Bolton Avoiding line, Bolton Loop, were but three names used for this short section which connected the Preston and Blackburn lines. It was used mainly by freight trip workings between the respective Bolton yards, Bullfield to the west, Halliwell, Craddock Lane, Bradshawgate etc., to the east. Excursions occasionally ran this way and it was not unknown for complete passenger trains to be turned around, thus avoiding time consuming light engine and empty stock movements within the station limits. Johnson Street Fork was finally taken out of use on the 25th January 1970.

Photos: M.S. Welch

Astley Bridge Branch

The track and bridge plans for the Astley Bridge branch were drawn up in June 1873 and signed by the Engineer Abraham Pilling. It was an undertaking entirely promoted by the LYR and formed a junction near Folds Road on the Tonge viaduct of the Bolton to Blackburn line running for 1 mile 184 yards where it reached the terminus alongside the Bolton to Blackburn turnpike road at Astley Bank. The statutory powers for its construction were contained within The Act for the Chatburn to Hellifield line. It cost £60,000 and was opened for all traffic on 15th October 1877. Although a passenger station was built and opened it must have seen little patronage as it ceased on the 1st October 1879, after running eight daily return trips into Bolton, averaging five passengers per day! The terminus remained in use for a further 84 years as goods station and coal depot, until the 4th September 1961 when it was used solely for condemned wagon storage up until 1964. Undoubtedly the focal point on the branch was at Halliwell with its three storey goods warehouse 300 ft. long by 50 ft. wide. This was later extended with what became known as the new Egyptian Cotton Warehouse, fitted with electrically operated lights, capstans and travelling cranes. Cotton appears to have become the main business of the branch a logic which was probably the thought behind the building of it. However, the construction of Back o'th Bank power station of the Bolton Corporation Electricity works in 1914 brought extra traffic as electric winding gear lifted coal wagons and discharged them into hoppers. A report in the *Bolton Journal & Guardian* of 18th January 1929 throws some interesting light on the operation of this important goods depot.

'Whenever a goods train starts down the branch a loud sounding bell commences to ring as soon as the train approaches within 100 yards of Halliwell Sidings. This particular alarm serves the double purpose of (a) warning the outside staff against possible danger and (b) preparing the indoor workers to handle the incoming traffic expeditiously.

As evening approaches 100 electric lights are switched on of varying intensity up to 1,000 candle power. This is to illuminate the entire installation at Halliwell'. In 1929 with a town still largely illuminated with gas light this would be sufficient a novelty to be emphasised. Replacement of horses with electrical capstans is also given special prominence. Apparently, power was relayed from Back o'th Bank. *'The only duty required of the capstan man, after having got his wagon rope in position, is to depress a pedal, thereby switching on current to an out-of-sight electrical motor, the capstan commences to revolve. In this interesting fashion, heavily laden goods wagons are shunted to and fro with the greatest of ease.'*

'It is almost bewildering to watch how within a stone's throw of these capstans other mechanical gadgets perform their allotted work, viz: 25 jiggers, friction cranes and lifts with a lifting capacity of 28 tons.'

The decline in use of the depot is directly related to that of cotton production from the 1950s onwards. Whilst the coal trains diminished as more coal merchants went over to deliveries by road, the Astley Bridge section was cut back to Ulleswater Street in 1963. Halliwell was now the terminus maintained by the needs of the power station until that too closed in 1979. This brought about the end of the branch with the closure of Halliwell on the 3rd August 1981. Although the junction box was switched out at the same time it was not demolished until 15th December 1982.

Craddock Lane sidings connection was removed on the 24th May 1965 and the signal box closed in the August of the same year. A private siding nearby to serve Harry Peers Steelworks was taken out of use on the 14th July 1960.

93. Astley Bridge Junction, 8th February 1964. From high above Turner Lane, a coal train from Burnden Sidings negotiates Astley Bridge Junction on its way to Halliwell. The Working Time Table of Freight Trains for 13th June to 18th September 1955 shows a single working from Burnden Sidings to Halliwell, departing 9.06am for a twelve minute journey – Saturdays Only – and possibly similar to this working seen here. In the week the train ran later, 10.44am departure on Mondays, 10.49 Tuesday to Friday. Astley Bridge Junction signal box, seen half way along the train, was rather precariously perched on girders suspended between the adjoining viaducts. It was a wooden structure with a 24 lever frame built in 1913 to replace an earlier Smith and Yardley box (18 levers) of 1875. The only subjects remaining today are a single section of track on the Blackburn line and a tree infested structure that served as Astley Bridge viaduct. These lofty structures provided a haven for many small businesses, with a predilection for scrap metal merchants. The yard below with its hand carts and assorted junk is a fascinating footnote of such occupation surviving on the periphery of the industrial heartland.

Photo: John Marshall

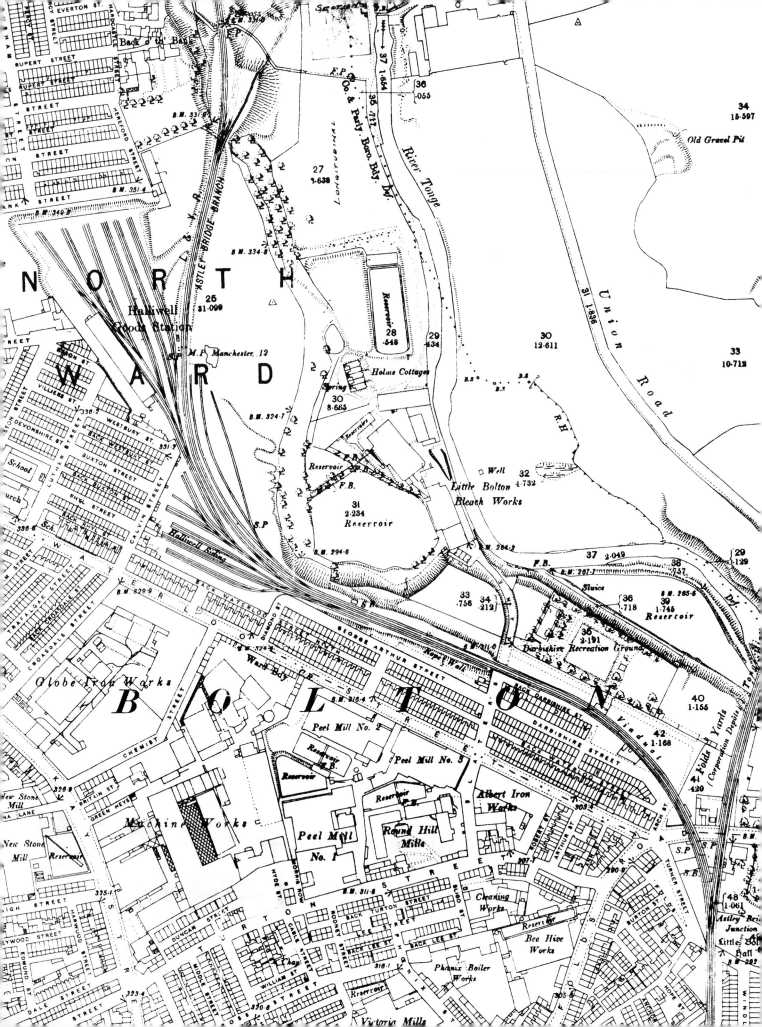

94. Halliwell Goods, Saturday 14th May 1960. Former L&YR 0-6-0 ST No. 51486 is seen here shunting the yard. The branch opened to Halliwell on the 12th February 1876, where in effect, the goods work on the line became concentrated to the extent of building the large cotton warehouse in the background. In the days of intensive production of surrounding mills, the densely populated neighbourhood had to live with the nocturnal echoes and clanking of buffers of wagons and from this engine and its class relatives. Referring once again to the freight time table mentioned previously, Halliwell was served mainly by trip workings from the other Bolton locations. During weekdays the following trains were booked:

ARRIVALS: 6.30am *(6.15 ex-Bullfield)*; 9.18am *(SO 9.6am ex-Burnden Junction)*; 10.55am *(MO ex-Burnden Junction)*, 11am *(MSX 10.45 ex-Burnden Junction)* 11.25am *(9.25 ex-Westhoughton)*; 11.40am *(8.45 ex-Bamfurlong)*; 11.50am *(SO 11.35 ex-Bullfield)*; 1.30pm *(1.20 ex-Bradshawgate – with empties)* 2.37pm *(SO 2.30 ex-Bradshawgate – with empties)*; 7.13pm *(SX 7.5pm ex-Bradshawgate – with empties)*;

DEPARTURES: 9.55am *(SX Sharlston, Yorks – with empties)* 11.45am *(MSX Light engine to Bullfield for 12.35pm to Horwich)* 11.53am *(Engine and Two Brakes to Hindley North)*; 12 noon *(SX Empties to Laisterdyke)*; 2.25pm *(SO Empties to Pontefract)*; 2.55pm *(SO Burnden Junction)*; 5.35pm *(SX Rose Hill Junction)*; 6.30pm *(SO Pontefract)*.

Other movements were made under local arrangements. The empty wagon trains to Yorkshire destinations indicate some use of coal from collieries east of the Pennines by the Central Electricity Authority plant at Bolton Power Station. Full wagons would have been 'tripped' in from the other Bolton yards. To illustrate how many workings were carried out by local arrangements, the nearby Craddock Lane Sidings supposedly had only one train booked to call, the 8.10am from Bullfield, which paid a twenty minute visit on its way up the Blackburn line with the 'bank shunt' pick up goods. Forty three minutes were allowed at Bromley Cross, twenty minutes at Turton and Edgeworth, and twenty five at Entwistle, before returning to Rose Hill Junction. The veteran engine seen here had been at Bolton for a few years but was now in the last months of its life, being withdrawn in the September. *Photo: John Marshall*

95. Astley Bridge, c.1960. Another Class 2F 0-6-0ST, No. 51408, shunts the yard at Astley Bridge in her role as Halliwell 'pilot'. Coal traffic was still in evidence at this time but the yard was increasingly being used to store wagons. The short lived passenger station was sited behind the engine, the approach being down a slight incline from Tippinge's Road. Once again, much use was made of the 'pilot' by local arrangement. The only booked working however left Halliwell at 7.45am being allowed five minutes for the journey to Astley Bridge. The same engine returned twenty five minutes later with a brake van. *Photo: N.R. Knight*

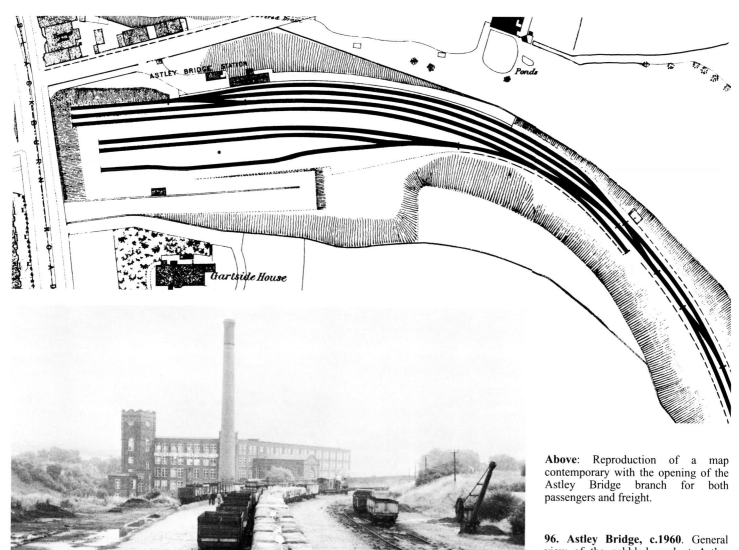

Above: Reproduction of a map contemporary with the opening of the Astley Bridge branch for both passengers and freight.

96. Astley Bridge, c.1960. General view of the cobbled yard at Astley Bridge terminus with, in the distance, the itinerant Saddle tank – seen in plate 95 – waiting for a decision to be made on its next move, probably alone with the brake van. The North End Spinning Co's Mill stands dominantly beyond the open ground at the side of the railway. It is a little hard to imagine that the crane to the right is, or was, capable of lifting a 10 ton load. The station site, mentioned previously, was the cleared area to the left. *Photo: N.R. Knight*

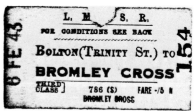

97. Astley Bridge, 27th June 1960. The houses of Elmfield Street have for many years occupied the site of Gartside House, although it is unlikely the view of Astley Bridge yard endeared it to the former landowners. A mixture of both operative and condemned wagons occupy the sidings, whilst the huge cooling tower of 'Back o'th Bank' power station stands prominently on the Bolton townscape. *Photo: John Marshall*

MANCHESTER, BLACKBURN, CLITHEROE, CHATBURN, GISBURN, and HELLIFIELD.—Lancashire and Yorkshire.

(Down — Week Days timetable grid with stations: Euston Station, 527 London dep., 535 (St. Pan.), Manchester (V.) dep., Salford, Pendleton, Bolton (Trin. St.), The Oaks, Bromley Cross, Turton and Edgworth, Entwistle, Spring Vale, Darwen, Lower Darwen, Blackburn arr./dep., Daisy Field, Wilpshire for Ribchester, Langho for Chester, Whalley, Clitheroe, Chatburn, Rimington, Gisburn, Newsholme, Hellifield arr., 620 Carlisle arr., 620 Edinbro', 620 Glasgow.)

Week Days—Continued.

NOTES.

a Stops on Tuesdays, Thursdays, and Saturdays.
b Except Thursdays and Saturdays.
c Stops on Tuesdays to take up for Carlisle and beyond.
d Stop if required to set down from London.
h Stops on Tuesdays when required to take up for North of Hellifield.
k Leaves 5 minutes earlier on Thursdays and Saturdays.
k Stops to take up.
z Broad Street.
s Saturdays only.

∗ Waverley Station.
† St. Enoch Station.
§ Citadel Station.

∗.∗ For SUNDAY TRAINS see page 768.

☞ For LOCAL TRAINS and Intermediate Stations between Manchester and Bolton, see page 774.

HELLIFIELD, GISBURN, CHATBURN, CLITHEROE, BLACKBURN, and MANCHESTER.—Lancashire and Yorkshire.

(Up — Week Days timetable grid with stations: St. Enoch Station, 621 Glasgow dep., 621 Edinbro' (Wav.), 621 Carlisle, Hellifield dep., Newsholme, Gisburn, Rimington, Chatburn, Clitheroe, Whalley, Langho, Wilpshire for Ribchester, Daisy Field, Blackburn arr./dep., Lower Darwen, Darwen, Spring Vale, Entwistle, Turton and Edgworth, Bromley Cross, The Oaks, Bolton arr., Pendleton, Salford, M'chester (Vic.) arr., 527 London (Euston) arr., 549 (St. Pan.).)

Week Days—Continued.

NOTES.

a Set down if required from Carlisle and North thereof.
b Stop if required to set down from North of Hellifield.
c Stops when required to take up for Derby and beyond.
d Stops if required to take up for Manchester.
f Stops when required to take up for Crewe and beyond.
g Stop if required to set down.
n Sunday night times.
h Sets down if required from Carlisle and beyond; also takes up for beyond Blackburn.
k Stops on Saturdays if required to take up.
s Sets down if required on Saturdays from beyond Blackburn.
o Stops if required to take up for London.
s Saturdays only.
v Stops to set down from Midland Line.
z Broad Street.
∗ Trinity Street.
§ Citadel Station.

☞ For LOCAL TRAINS and Intermediate Stations between Bolton and Manchester, see page 775.

L. & Y.

MANCHESTER, BLACKBURN, CLITHEROE, CHATBURN, GISBURN, and HELLIFIELD.—Lancashire and Yorkshire.

Down. — Sundays. | Up. — Sundays.

(Sunday timetable grids for both directions with the same station lists.)

n Sets down if required from Carlisle and North thereof.
i Saturday night.
n Stop to set down.
∗ Trinity Street.

☞ For LOCAL TRAINS and Intermediate Stations between Manchester and Bolton, see pages 774 and 775.

MANCHESTER, ASHTON, and STALYBRIDGE.—Lancashire and Yorkshire.

Down. — Week Days. — Sundays.

(Stations: Victoria Station, Manchester, Miles Platting, Park, Clayton Bridge, Droylsden, Ashton (Charlestown), Stalybridge.)

Up. — Week Days. — Sundays.

(Stations: Stalybridge, Ashton (Charlestown), Droylsden, Clayton Bridge, Park, Miles Platting, Manchester (Vic.).)

The Oaks

The interesting thing about this station that sets it apart from all others in the district is that it was built on private land with access along a private road which led to a large house alongside the River Tonge. It seems certain that the station was conceded to on behalf of this house and its owner. To ensure privacy it was not named as would normally have been appropriate, otherwise the nearby community of Bradshaw would have found itself on the railway map. When stations were built on large country estates the landowner often had a great deal of influence upon their design and appearance. Although the original building seen in the photographs can hardly be described as ornamental, it does suggest some kind of distinction. The first station was probably a penurious affair, barely adequate. Some rebuilding was undertaken in the 1880's but it was 1901 which saw the most drastic changes in the form of long sweeping platforms and a footbridge crossing three tracks as well as some additional buildings. At that time Bolton station itself was undergoing a drastic rebuilding, so perhaps the area near this station was envisaged as becoming part of the new suburbia that was growing up around Tonge Moor. However, the electric tramways were soon to supply that particular need and freight traffic never seems to have been catered for at 'The Oaks' at all. On the 27th May 1920 a lattice timber bridge nearby, by the name of Boggart Hole Bridge, was renewed.

Like many rural stations, The Oaks was in an area reasonably well served by other forms of public transport, whilst housing development was to be another two decades away. Nonetheless, the passenger train service was no different than other stations on the line, and the five minute journey to or from Bolton Trinity Street would no doubt have been welcomed these days. The summer timetable prior to closure on 6th November 1950 was somewhat better than that of forty years earlier. Passengers heading south fared well, with fourteen trains during weekdays, no less than five before nine o'clock, at 6.07am, 6.57, 7.20, 8.05 and 8.47. Northbound, there were twelve trains daily, with eight of those being equally shared between the evening and morning peaks. The loop lines also gave refuge to slower moving freights climbing for the seven miles to Sough.

98. The Oaks, 16th July 1965. From the front end of a Blackburn bound Diesel Multiple Unit we continue our climb north. In the distance we see the brick built wartime (WW2) A.R.P. signal box. The exact date of opening has not been clarified, but records exist indicating that the new 'The Oaks Station' signal box was being built to replace Birtenshaw and The Oaks signal box, in November 1942. The existing 'Oaks' signal box at the time was immediately south of the level crossing at the Bolton end of the station, down side. The box seen here was closed on the 25th October 1966, the loops being taken out of use on the same day. The twin gabled building to the right contained the Station Master's House together with Lamp & Porters Room, General Waiting Room and Ladies Waiting Room for the Up (south bound) platform. *Photo: P.E. Baughan*

99. The Oaks, November 1902. The Oaks, totally rebuilt from the original station of 1859, and ready to receive traffic alongside the new platforms. It is difficult to visualize how the station could have continued to operate through this upheaval – was the earlier station on the south side of the level crossing? Minor alterations to the first station were completed in 1886 when a timber waiting room was added to the northbound platform. Included in this proposal was a stone building containing office and waiting room facilities, located on the opposite side and near to existing buildings. The enlarged station seen here was completed in 1903 and included the Up and Down loop lines. The platforms were now 200 yards long with timber built waiting rooms on the Down side, left, in this view towards Blackburn. The footbridge was typical of a design used widely on the Lancashire and Yorkshire Railway.
Photo: John Marshall

100. The Oaks, 3rd July 1962. Bowling down from Sough summit with the 7.10am service from Hellifield to Manchester Victoria is 'Crab' 2-6-0 No. 42728, piloting one of the named Class 5MT 4-6-0's, No. 45154 *Lanarkshire Yeomanry*, at the time both Newton Heath engines. This particular working, with minor variations in timings, had operated for many years and provided a fast service into Manchester for the stations between Hellifield and Blackburn. Leaving Blackburn, the train called at Darwen, its only other intermediate stop before Bolton, to then run express to Salford. At the end of the 1962 summer timetable, passenger services were withdrawn from the stations between Blackburn and Hellifield, thus bringing an end to this useful link. A truncated service from Blackburn continued to run to the same timings. The Oaks station had by this time been closed for over ten years. *Photo: John Marshall*

Bromley Cross

Some three miles from Bolton and just under half way on the climb from Bradshawgate Tunnel to Walton's Sidings, we come across the neat little stone built station of Bromley Cross. It was opened in 1859 to serve the local village of that name. Beyond the reach of the local tramway system, Bromley Cross Station had a rural significance that has maintained its stance to the present day. Local bleach works and mills prospered in the district, resulting in a capacious goods yard at the north end of the station. From the mid-18th century there was an enormous increase in the demand for building stone for mills, houses and civic buildings. Numerous quarries in the area rose to the occasion and continued expansion was only checked in any significant degree by the volume supply of Accrington Brick from 1875 onwards. Furthermore, when the line was opened in the 1840s the area between Bolton and Darwen was littered with small coal workings which ultimately became uneconomic as improved pumping machinery and techniques enabled deeper seams to develop in other areas like those around Wigan and Manchester.

101. Bromley Cross, c.1905. The completed station as seen in the early years of the twentieth century, with signal box, goods shed, and facing platforms. Much development has taken place to the north of the station in recent years, with a car park and housing covering much of the goods shed area and former yard. However, it remains to this day as an example of the semi-rural/country stations which vanished in such large numbers during the nineteen sixties. One remarkable feature of the early stations was the large bell-jar type gas lamp with the name of the station etched on the glass. Several are to be seen here. Note also the timber shelter on the down side, probably a later edition than the stone building opposite. The signal box adjacent to the level crossing is another fine example of a fast diminishing railway structure as modern equipment reduces the need for such buildings. The brick built box is a Smith and Yardley type of 1875, originally provided with a 20 lever frame which was replaced in 1902 by a 28 lever L&Y, the enlargement being due to the quadrupling of the line. The frame was further modified in 1977, twelve levers being removed. *Photo: Heydey Publishing Co*

102. Bromley Cross, 16th July 1965. Sunlight and empty platforms on this summer day in 1965 as the DMU on which the photographer is travelling approaches Bromley Cross on its journey to Blackburn. The somewhat austere and weather-worn appearance of the goods shed tends to reflect the lack of activity in the yard. However, Bromley Cross retained its public freight facilities longer than most, closure not taking place until the 24th July 1967. The daily pick-up goods was known by the Bolton men as the 'bank shunt', the 'bank' referring to the climb out of the town towards Blackburn. The outward trip left Bullfield at 8.10am and first of all called at Craddock Lane on its way north before spending the best part of three quarters of an hour in Bromley Cross yard. After going to Turton, the train called again on its way back to Bolton, being allowed another eighteen minutes to pick up any relevant wagons. *Photo: P.E. Baughan*

103. Bromley Cross, 23rd May 1961. At first glance, LNER built Class B1 No. 61298 looks to be performing an outstanding feat with what appears to be an exceedingly long train of vans bound for Ancoats, Manchester. The facts, however, were less impressive when discovering that the train usually consisted of empty vehicles being returned from Glasgow. An interesting aside about the presence of B1's in Lancashire was that in the mid 1950's Agecroft depot had to exchange six of their Stanier 'Black Fives' for the same number of B1 engines from Leicester Shed. The Agecroft men were less than impressed with the arrangement whilst the Leicester men were perfectly happy. The former exerted every conceivable amount of effort before they finally got their Class 5's back!

Photo: John Marshall

104. Bromley Cross, 18th April 1963. To the right are the rugged little buildings of the Blackburn, Darwen & Bolton Railway. Opened in 1848 and built with stone from the Ouzle Nest quarry nearby, the buildings stand to this day to provide a welcome change to the functional styles of modern railway architecture. The original platform height is clearly evident as are features of the quadrupled section of line extending northwards and completed in 1903. The extra capacity, as well as requiring extra levers in the signal box, resulted in another signal box, Bromley Cross North, a wooden L&Y structure of 1902 with a 32 lever frame which closed in 1954.

Photo: G.J. Biddle

Turton & Edgeworth

Two miles beyond Bromley Cross the line continues its climb towards the windswept summit of Cranberry Moss. Originally known as Chapeltown, its name was changed to Turton in 1877 before becoming Turton & Edgeworth in 1891. However, with the mill close by the community of Chapeltown, it must have known intense activity at some stage. The Lancashire Fusiliers camped close by during the 1914–18 war and from the station's low platforms, soldiers crowded into railway coaches for their eventual rendezvous with destiny on the Straits of Gallipoli. On a lighter note the Royal Train paused on its journey one night and was secretly shunted into the sidings at Turton. The Royal personage using the train was none other than HRH The Queen Mother who, on the following morning, decided to leave the train for a stroll, calling upon a local farmhouse. The reaction of the person who opened that farmhouse door must have been little short of sheer bewilderment. Her Majesty stayed for a short chat before returning to the train.

105. Turton, 16th July 1965. There was an assurance to James Kay, resident of Turton Tower, that no station would be built within 300 yards of the house, also that his driveway would be imposingly contained against the incursion of the railway. Thus, the crenellated 'tudor' style, pointed arch bridge appeared to carry Mr. Kay's road over the railway. An even more elevated view can be obtained from the larger of the two turrets. Nowadays, further encroachment of the vegetation hides the bridge's attractive feature somewhat. Many landowners in the early days took an unsympathetic view of the railways and one wonders if that view was maintained when the line became an access route to both London and Scotland. This view again is from a northbound train. *Photo: P.E. Baughan*

106. Turton & Edgeworth, 2nd February 1963. Ex W.D. 'Austerity' 2-8-0 No. 90429 a probable Brindle Heath–Carlisle goods 'up the bank' to Entwistle. Footplate crews of tender engines preferred to work up this line tender first as they would be travelling slowly up when the wind was blowing into the cab causing less discomfort. This particular engine, Wakefield based, was a regular visitor to Bolton on the trans-Pennine coal trains. It was also popular with Bolton men, having minor refinements such as padded seats in the cab. The day after this turn of duty, 90429 was on its way back to Wakefield in charge of a Kearsley–Healey Mills working. The engines used on banking duties occasionally included ex-works or trial engines recently outshopped from Horwich.

Photo: John Marshall

107. Turton & Edgeworth, 18th April 1963. No snow in this view but a
continued on next page

107 continued

scene still recovering from the harsh winter of 1963. The station had been closed to passengers for just over two years but was still dealing with coal traffic in the sidings to the rear of the building. This facility was withdrawn on 28th December 1964, the connections to and from the sidings being clipped out of use, pending removal, on 15th February 1965. The structures here date from three different periods. The signal box was an LNWR type 5 structure with a Lancashire and Yorkshire Railway frame, the hybrid dating from 1927. It replaced a Smith and Yardley 20 lever signal box of 1876. The footbridge bearing on two stone piers, was an L&Y 'standard' type, the word standard very loosely applied for the company had several over the years. The platform fronting the burnt out station building was indeed low, similar to Bromley Cross. *Photo: G.J. Biddle*

108. (Above-right) Turton & Edgeworth, c.1964. Again we see a post-fire view of the original 1848 buildings with the large goods shed behind. The rugged stone and cobbled platform typifies north country style. Nowadays largely overgrown, a single track remains to serve Manchester/Bolton to Blackburn services.

Photo: Bolton Evening News

109. Turton, c.1915. An undated photograph overlooking an area near Turton. What is known is that the Lancashire Fusiliers marched to and embarked for Gallipoli from Turton Station, note the tents across the background. Scenes such as this were fairly commonplace around the country, particularly North Wales, but rarely photographed. For those interested in rolling stock, the 'special gunpowder vans' are to a specification involving modification of a covered goods van design. The vehicles seen here are thought to be converted vans, which externally involved alterations to the roof and doors.

Photo: B.C. Lane collection

110. Turton & Edgeworth, c.1950. This shows the platform reconstructed with concrete components to an LMS design, and adopted later by British Railways, and probably made at Newton Heath. Other standardized items include the sectional wooden buildings and LMS poster boards, one of which at this end of the building possesses a 'Hawkeseye' pattern station name sign. Staggered platforms were often arranged for the convenience of train working where stations had level crossings, as this allowed the train to clear the crossing as it stopped and have the gates closed behind it. As mentioned elsewhere, Turton closed to passengers on 5th February 1961.

Photo: Bolton Evening News,

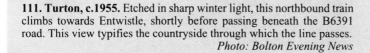

111. Turton, c.1955. Etched in sharp winter light, this northbound train climbs towards Entwistle, shortly before passing beneath the B6391 road. This view typifies the countryside through which the line passes.
Photo: Bolton Evening News

Entwistle

Our journey to the next station along the line, has seen an ascent almost to 737ft above sea level. The photographic scenes portray the open and somewhat exhilarating location of Entwistle Station on a bright winter's day under an ice blue sky. The station footpath leads directly into the tempting prominence of the local hostelry, neat in its heavy stone and bright shining rooms. Since the station's opening in 1848 additional lines produced the need for an island platform and goods sidings. An example of this line's openness and vulnerability occurred as recent as 18th July 1964 when the town of Bolton faced the onslaught of rain that fell as if a curtain of water had suddenly descended. In only fifteen minutes 2.21 inches fell and caused such extensive damage that all Bolton and Blackburn trains had to be diverted via Chorley.

Between Entwistle and Spring Vale is the summit of the line at Waltons Sidings, immediately before Sough tunnel. Bolton fireman Joe Strickleton had a particular dislike of Sough and when trying one wintry morning to get a Thomson B1 through with a Carlisle–Ancoats goods train for over an hour, it slipped and restarted time and time again before reaching Entwistle and the relieving freshness of descent.

112. Entwistle, 16th July 1965. Still continuing the climb of 1 in 72/74 that commenced after Bradshawgate tunnel, our DMU, from which several views forward have been taken, approaches Entwistle station. The summit of the line at Waltons Siding (800ft) lies ahead and this view shows clearly how the quadrupling affected the station after its completion in 1904. *Photo: P.E. Baughan*

113. Entwistle, 3rd December 1965. This view perhaps depicts Entwistle's true character, the raw open wastes of winter with the signal box standing **continued over**

113 continued
defiantly on its steel frame. Not surprisingly, it was not a coveted turn of duty for the signalman as the box had a good number of rugs and carpets to exclude every possible draught. From the visibility point of view, one could not ask for anything better. At one time a narrow gauge railway connected the station with a quarry a half mile away. A cable worked system also provided a method of movement of goods to and from a mill in the valley below.

114. (This page – Top) Entwistle, c.1910. The enlarged station in the years shortly after the quadrupling of the line between here and Waltons Siding. A bustling goods yard and all the features of an expanding railway are evident. The new works completely changed the face of the station. The Up (southbound) platform, located on the site of the signal box, was removed, the down (northbound) platform becoming the up with a new line positioned round the back to re-form the station as an island platform type. The two lines beneath the newly constructed signal box were designated up and down fast. The box, as seen here, was erected in 1904 on a steel gantry and was an L&Y all wood structure with a 60 lever frame. It replaced a Smith and Yardley box of 1876 which contained 20 levers. Note the sweeping reverse curves of the line leading up to Waltons Siding and the Sough Tunnel at Whittlestone Head. Beyond the valley the heights reach impressively up to Edgeworth Moor. The landscape is a continual reminder that this rail link was hard wrought from the terrain.
Photo: Heydey Publishing Co. Ltd

115. (This page – Centre) Entwistle, 6th July 1968. Perhaps the perfect setting of a hill country station, although not quite what it seems at first glance. Rationalisation and decay have become the byword. The signal box had closed a few weeks previously (26th May) and the fast lines taken out of use. Note all the signal posts north of the station totally devoid of their arms. The remaining lines, those serving the island platform, were re-named main lines. This somewhat remote spot retained railway staff until July 1971 when economy measures resulted in the withdrawal of that facility. The goods yard had closed on the 2nd November 1959. *Photo: G.J. Biddle*

116. (This page – Lower) Entwistle, 3rd December 1965. Looking back towards Bolton, the snow having come early that year. The building seen between the chimney stacks of the station was the local hostelry and probably served the station for accommodation during the 19th century. Much has happened in the
continued next page

116 continued

period since this photograph was taken, culminating in the survival of just a single track – to the left of the building – and platform with rudimentary shelter. Almost everything else within the railway boundary has returned to nature.

117. (Above) Entwistle Viaduct, 16th July 1965. A Stanier Class 5MT with a fitted freight, having breasted the summit at Waltons Siding, will now no doubt coast down into Bolton. The area is very reminiscent of the famous Settle to Carlisle route some forty miles north of here. Note the check rails on the left hand track situated between the running lines. The track to the right has bullhead rail with a cast chair able to accommodate the check rail.
Photo: P.E. Baughan

118. (Centre) Entwistle Viaduct, c.1910. A Blackburn bound train headed by Lancashire & Yorkshire 'radial' 2-4-2 tank engine crosses over the wooded valley in the early years of the century. Beneath it the expanse of Wayoh Reservoir village of Edgeworth beyond. Only some six miles from Bolton town centre and there is the fullest experience of Pennine grandeur. The structure was built of stone, had nine arches and was 120 feet at its highest point. Each of the spans or openings was 50 feet.
Photo: Heydey Publishing Co. Ltd

119. Sough Tunnel, n.d. Following the long climb from Bolton, the gradient suddenly changes to 1 in 69/75 as Sough Tunnel is entered for 1 mile 255 yards of darkness beneath Cranberry Moss. The enclosure of the sheer rock wall typifies the windswept nature of the terrain of rocky outcrops and tough moorland grasses and plants. The plain tunnel portal here at the south end is in marked contrast to the turreted entrance at the Blackburn end. *Photo: LGRP courtesy David & Charles*

West of Bolton

120. (Left) Bolton West, n.d. A piece of vintage L&Y signalling, this underhung bracket signal, adjacent to the Lostock end of platform three, carried the home signals controlling the through line and subsequent access to the Down lines to Bullfield and Lostock. It can also be seen in plates 14 and 38. *Photo: LYRS collection*

121. (Above) Bolton West, September 1954. Over fifty years after their introduction, these Lancashire and Yorkshire electro-pneumatic signals continued to serve well. The gantry carried the 'Up' signals, the 'distant' arm (lower left) being for Bradshawgate via the Johnson Street Fork. This view from above Great Moor Street tunnel adjacent to the town's other station, shows the effects of the quadrupling completed in 1905, the original alignment to the left, new to the right. Dawes Street is carried on the bridge behind the signal gantry. *Photo: G.J. Biddle*

122. Deane Clough. This view towards Bolton from Deane Clough bridge shows Class 5 4-6-0 No. 44782 with an excursion train bound for Blackpool. The Bolton to Lostock widening scheme completed in 1898 enabled quadrupling of the route but it was not just a simple addition of the two new lines, several structures requiring total reconstruction to accommodate the new alignment. Although Croal Mill still forms part of the Bolton skyline this section has subsequently reverted to two lines, and Deane Clough signal box, a 24 lever structure of 1900, closed on 26th September 1965 following the limited introduction of colour light signalling between Bullfield West and Lostock. *Photo: N.R. Knight*

123. Lostock, c.1964. A 'Stanier' 2-6-4 tank engine, carrying a freight headcode, makes its way leisurely along the Down slow line towards Lostock Junction with a short train of empty mineral wagons. Driver and fireman appear to be taking advantage of a turn that can hardly be described as taxing. *Photo: N.R. Knight*

124. Lostock Water Troughs. Deane Clough, between Bolton and Lostock Junction, was the site of water troughs installed by the Lancashire and Yorkshire Railway following the quadrupling of the section of line. To the left of the picture is the water tank house and pumping machinery, and judging by the exhaust of escaping steam, a steam driven pump. The elegant gantry carried 'distant' signals for Lostock Junction where the Wigan and Preston routes diverge. The two lines to the left are the Up fast (outer) and Up slow. Occasionally the parallel running lines would create an interesting visual experience. The author vividly remembers taking a leisurely view from a carriage window as a 'Stanier' 2-6-4 tank gradually overtook a 'Black Five' along this stretch. Neck and neck like charging horses with the latter engine's driving wheels spinning with indignation as it was passed, only recovering its loss by speeding through Lostock Junction, whilst its opponent was forced to stop. There were ten sets of water troughs on the L&Y system, six of which, Lostock being one, were heated during frosty weather.

Photo: National Railway Museum

Lostock Junction

The original station on the Bolton and Preston Railway was at Lostock Lane, a little further north, but with the opening of the Liverpool & Bury in 1848, a junction station was the obvious recourse. The level crossing to the east of Rumworth Road bridge required extra vigilance as the service on both lines was intensive, sufficiently so that the Board of Trade eventually forced the LYR's hand and a bridge, together with approach roads, was put in. The bridge and booking office with stairways to platforms was opened on 26th July 1887.

The station at Lostock, not surprisingly, expanded as a result of the local commerce which originally could have been little more than farming. With the building of Heaton's Mill in the late 19th century and the opening of the de Havilland Propeller Factory on 11th August 1937, the area took on a more expansive interest. With the quadrupling of the Bolton to Lostock section the station was completely resignalled. A large goods shed was built east of the station in 1899 and a 90 lever box installed, more sidings being added in 1914–18. To supplement the local population trains would bring in additional workforce for both these companies, not to mention the needs of the nearby special childrens school.

A most spectacular event at Lostock Junction on the 17th July 1920 was a collision between a Bolton bound train from Wigan, which was hauled by a 2-4-2 radial tank, weighing 55 tons 19 cwts, with five bogie passenger carriages of 119 tons 7 cwts which ran into the 2.05pm Bolton to Preston comprising eight bogie passenger carriages and a milk van and weighing 192 tons 12 cwts. All vehicles but one were gas lit, the exception being an electrically lit one. Mercifully there was no outbreak of fire but the front two coaches of the Wigan train telescoped although they were locked and empty. Four passengers were killed including one that died three days later. Ten were seriously injured and 135 had minor injuries and shock. Some of these people simply left the train, walked across the fields and went home. The accident was caused because of the mistaken conclusion by the Wigan train driver that he had a clear signal but did not check thoroughly. It has also to be admitted that the particular signal was not as obviously sited as would be ideal.

125. Lostock Junction, post 1887. There is a clean look about the booking office on the bridge in this view west, suggesting that the particular building, together with stairways, was comparatively new. The cottage in the 'vee' of the junction might at first appear to be an incomprehensible location but it has to be remembered that this was the accommodation for a level crossing keeper from the early days who was responsible for attending the gates and overseeing the safe passage of crossing users. The crossing was located immediately behind the cottage and passed in front of the 'Junction Inn', seen here on the left. It then continued across Middle Brook by means of a stone bridge and on to the village before reaching Deane. When the bridges were built over the two lines, they rendered the crossing redundant, the diverted road being located slightly to the west of the old alignment. The building of bridges to replace level crossings was by now commonplace throughout the country, probably at the insistence of the Board of Trade, which enforced companies to provide alternative crossings when rail and road usage had become too regular to control safely.

Photo: Bolton Evening News

126. Lostock Junction, 1st July 1965. Capacious goods yard facilities for such a rural location, particularly the extensive goods warehouse. The yard was extended during the WW1 period, doubtless wartime trade for the mill and later the de Havilland aircraft factory, in what was originally a minor village station. Passenger services were withdrawn from the station on 7th November 1966 but subsequent residential development in the area resulted in a new station, Lostock, serving trains on the Preston line. *Photo: G.J. Biddle*

127. Lostock Junction, 1st July 1965. The combined but somewhat unusual, booking office and water tank on the overbridge at Lostock. The Preston line is beneath the bridge to the left, Wigan line beneath the nearside parapet.
Photo: G.J. Biddle

128. Lostock Junction, c.1964. An expansive view of the mill with a BR Standard class locomotive taking the Wigan/Liverpool route whilst an Up working crosses to the fast line. The goods yard had been closed on the 9th September 1963 and the tracks are quickly becoming covered by vegetation. This view towards Bolton is from the Lostock Lane overbridge.
Photo: Bolton Evening News

129. Lostock Junction, 2nd June 1965. Stanier 2-cylinder Class 4 locomotive No. 42647, a Wigan (8F) based engine, slows down to call at Lostock Junction with a Rochdale to Southport train. To the rear of the train we can see how the eastbound Wigan line forms a junction with the Up fast line in front of the signal box. Considering that the station was within eighteen months of closure, it enjoyed a good train service with upwards of thirty five in each direction calling, the majority at Wigan line platforms.

Photo: John Marshall

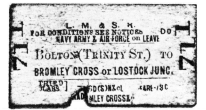

130. Lostock Sidings, 25th April 1962. The marshalling sidings on the Wigan line to the west of Lostock Junction were extensive, the combined capacity of both Lostock Marshalling and Chew Moor Traffic sidings being in excess of 1250 wagons. This view from behind Lostock Sidings South signal box gives some idea of the extent of the site as ex-LNWR 'G2' 0-8-0 No. 49438 passes with an eastbound freight train. The site of the sidings was laid out in the form of a triangular junction between the Wigan and Preston lines, with land and bridge over a diverted Middle Brook prepared for a northerly connection. In the event, the sidings, thought to have been opened in 1917, only operated from the southern end and controlled from Lostock Sidings South signal box, an all timber structure with a 25 lever frame. Progressive reduction of train sorting activities had seen the importance of places such as Chew Moor and Lostock diminish and following a period in which they were latterly used for wagon storage, the siding along with the signal box fulfilled their last function on 2nd April 1967.

Photo: F. Dean

Westhoughton

Known as West Houghton in the early days of the Liverpool & Bury Rly. Originally, there had been a station by the name of Chew Moor between Lostock and Westhoughton but this was closed in 1852. The sidings at this point had initially been conceived as a connecting line between the Preston and Wigan route, but it remained unrealised.

131. Westhoughton, c.1860. This early view shows what is possibly a Bolton bound train from Liverpool, note the interesting assembly of 4 wheel carriages. Of interest is the single storeyed end of the station building nearest the camera which was built on in later years.

Photo: Westhoughton Library

132. Westhoughton, 1st July 1965. Opened as a Liverpool & Bury Railway station in 1848, it was one of a number of functional but unimpressive station buildings in the Bolton area. The extensive accommodation probably reflected not so much the passenger traffic, but more the freight side and the numerous groups of goods and marshalling yards nearby, namely Chew Moor and Lostock Sidings.

Photo: G.J. Biddle

133. Westhoughton, 18th August 1964. High summer, and passing a Westhoughton hardly changed in time, Stanier 2-cylinder 2-6-4 tank No. 42631 clanks lazily back to depot. This particular engine had been based at Wigan L&Y shed (27D) for many years. Upon closure there it was transferred to Springs Branch from where it was withdrawn in 1964.

Photo: H.B. Priestley

134. Crow Nest Junction, n.d. A feature of the railway network that has lost a great deal of interesting diversity are the expansive country junctions. One outstanding example, albeit without station, was Crow Nest Junction between Bolton and Wigan. This view from the Bolton/ Westhoughton line towards Wigan shows the L&Y signal box of 1920 before a signalling and track remodelling scheme was put in hand towards the end of the Second World War. The 'Atherton' line bears to the left, whilst the pair to the right curved north out of the picture towards Hindley and Blackrod Branch Junction before continuing to meet the Preston line at Horwich Fork Junction. In more recent times, dequadrification of the Atherton line in 1966 ultimately reduced Crow Nest to merely a double line junction. A new British Railways standard signal box replaced the structure seen here from the 1st October 1972.

135. Crow Nest Junction, 22nd April 1967. This view west from the Wigan direction shows the junction in probably its most complete form. Tracks to the left of the box sub-divide again for Horwich and Bolton respectively whilst those to the right form the quadrupled section – fast lines to the left, slow to the right – to Atherton and Manchester.

Photo: H.B. Priestley

136. Daisy Hill: Dobbs Brow Junction, 24th August 1954. The Lancashire and Yorkshire Railway Company route from Pendleton to Hindley, the 'Atherton' line was built on a generous scale, the four track formation enabling maximum capacity for both passenger and freight services. Stations at Pendlebury, Swinton, Moorside and Walkden were constructed with an island platform between the slow lines. Pendleton and Atherton had platforms serving all four lines although the latter additionally had a bay at the Manchester end. The view here shows Stanier Class 5 No. 45225 negotiating the 40mph junction at Dobbs Brow with the 4.20pm Manchester Victoria to Blackpool train. First booked stop out of Manchester was Preston before running express to Lytham and then all stations to Blackpool Central. Dobbs Brow Junction signal box, an all wood structure of 1904, contained a 56 lever frame. Its importance declined rapidly when the fast lines between Pendleton and Crow Nest Junction were taken out of use in 1966. Closure of the short stretch to Hindley and Blackrod Branch Junction on 9th September 1968 witnessed the loss of its junction status, with the ultimate demise coming on 26th January 1969.

Photo: W.S. Garth

Horwich and Blackrod

Some three miles north west of Lostock Junction on the Preston line, the Hindley and Blackrod Branch came in from the left at Horwich Fork Junction after passing stations at Hilton House and Dicconson Lane. The short branch had provided a facility for through running from the Bolton–Wigan line at Hindley, via Blackrod and Chorley, to Preston and Blackburn, routes independent of the LNWR's main line on the west coast.

The Act for the section from Blackrod to Hindley, and from Blackrod to Horwich received the Royal Assent in 1864. Goods traffic began on the Hindley line on 15th July 1868 whilst the passenger trains began running a short time after on 14th September 1868. Effectively it was a route from Wigan to Chorley for local traffic. A branch to Horwich was opened on 14th February 1870. Hitherto, Blackrod had been called Horwich Road, which, for a time, was known as Horwich & Blackrod Junction until 1888 by which time the clear distinction between the two communities was made. Obviously the decision to build the new locomotive works of the Lancashire & Yorkshire Railway at the end of an obscure branch would prove momentous, but it did not create Horwich in the manner of a Crewe or Wolverton. The town already had 3,500 inhabitants working in cotton goods and bleaching although the railway unquestionably made its mark on the town with which it became synonymous.

The building of the works began on the 14th February 1885 and

it eventually opened in 1887. At the same time, a fork line avoiding Blackrod was opened to give direct access to Bolton and Manchester over Red Moss.

The impact of Horwich-produced locomotives and rolling stock etc., on the LYR, LMS and British Railways is the subject of a history in itself and much has already been written in detail. A large proportion of the locomotives seen in the pages of this book emanated from its workshops.

On the branch, two junctions with the works railway complex were made over which traffic was considerable. For instance, the method used for testing recently shopped locomotives in the 1930s was for them to leave Horwich at 10.40am, run via Chorley to Blackburn, then from Blackburn to Bolton over the Johnson Street Fork to join the Bolton and Preston line and arrive back on Horwich at 12.16pm. In the reverse direction locos could leave at 13.25, returning at 15.13.

Branch working alternated on the Blackrod to Horwich service and was an obvious choice for steam railmotors. The local service to Chorley, Bolton and Manchester was shared with the Radcliffe–Bradley Fold–Horwich workings which became the last haunt of the LYR steam railmotors, operating until 1947.

Decline of the works' status parallels that of the eclipse of steam traction. The last steam locomotive to be built there was Class 4 2-6-0 No. 76099, finished on 28th November 1957 and allocated to Corkerhill (Glasgow).

With the formation of the Workshops Division of BR in 1963, Horwich was designated a Wagon Repair Works. As a BREL unit it continued to overhaul Electric Multiple Units, Wagons, Service Vehicles, simultaneously diversifying into the production of PVC nylon and polyester sheets, laminated springs and iron castings.

137. Horwich, 1965. This view of the Up platform serving eastbound trains. The station was originally called Horwich Road, before becoming Blackrod Junction when the branch was opened to Horwich on 1st July 1868 for goods and 14th February 1870 for passengers. Undoubtedly the station acquired a special importance when Horwich Works opened in 1887. There is a rugged attractiveness about this 1843 building, enhanced somewhat with the addition of the large stone built goods shed which provided covered transhipment facilities for a proportion of the 101 wagons it was possible to accommodate in the yard. In common with many other stations, its platforms have been raised utilizing standard concrete components.
Photo: John Marshall

138. Horwich, 1962. View from a Preston bound train of the Up platform looking back towards Bolton. Just visible to the extreme right is the wooden stairway and bridge over the rail access to the goods shed. The signals serve both main (left) and branch (Hindley and Blackrod – right). There is little sign of activity in the goods shed, perhaps the shape of things to come, goods facilities being withdrawn on 1st August 1963.
Photo: G.H. Platt

139. Blackrod, 1947. The Horwich branch platform at Blackrod with a recently rebuilt platform wall of standard concrete components. At the time the motor train service comprised twelve trains during weekdays from Horwich to Blackrod but fifteen in the opposite direction. Other trains calling at Blackrod included the Workmens Special at 6.25am from Leyland, and the 7.14 departure from R.O.F. Halt (Chorley). An empty Rail Motor and Light Engine (coupled) left Bolton Shed (Mondays only) to work the 6.00am Horwich to Bolton service, returning with the 6.08am to Blackrod.
Photo: LGRP
courtesy David & Charles

140. Blackrod, 24th September 1965. A BR Standard Class 2MT 2-6-2 tank No. 84025 moves away from the branch platform with the 4.57pm – ex-Horwich – to Chorley (arr 5.09). The working had a long history of running to these timings, this occasion being the last due to withdrawal of passenger train services from the branch after the last train on the following day. The signal box to the right of the engine is Blackrod Junction, a structure dating from 1891 and for some unknown reason, possessing a base 15 feet wide instead of the usual twelve. Since the beginning of 1990 it has been the fringe box of the Manchester Piccadilly signalling panel. *Photo: P.E. Baughan*

141. Blackrod, 31st March 1964. The branch push-pull set, utilizing an ex LMS vehicle, waits in the platform after arriving from Horwich. In all probability it is timed to provide a connection with the Bolton bound train approaching from the right. Note the cobbled ramp, a legacy from the original platform. *Photo: G.J. Biddle*

The Horwich to Blackrod rail-motor, or motor train as it was sometimes called, appeared in numerous guises over the years. On this page are but three versions that appeared at some stage over a period spanning three decades.

142. Blackrod, 1933. A Sentinel-Cammell Steam rail coach in service with the LMS at Blackrod on the Horwich branch in 1933. This particular vehicle, No. 4149, was one of a batch of 12 built in 1927 with a 2-cylinder engine and chain drive transmission. Two more rail cars, No. 4349 and 44, were built on 6-cylinder engines with gear transmission, although externally they were similar in appearance to the twelve in existence. Most, if not all, worked on the Northern Division of the LMS in Scotland. The LMS renumbered the railcar 29907 in 1933 although it was withdrawn from service in 1935, along with the other eleven of the particular batch.

Photo: LGRP
courtesy David & Charles

143. Blackrod, c.1937. One of the Lancashire and Yorkshire built Rail Motors built to a design of Hughes and introduced in 1906. It was the last of the sets to survive (see plate 22). The tiny 0-4-0 tank engines could be paired with any of the coaches built for this type of work, repairs making it necessary on occasions. Depending on direction of travel, the Driver performed his duties from either the footplate or in the driving compartment of the coach, operating the 'train' through a system of wires and levers. *Photo: Bill Lees*

144. Blackrod, c.1952. A scene from times past, the two coach Horwich rail-motor in the branch platform at Blackrod. These ex-L&Y 2-4-2 tank engines operated the service in the 1950's when this picture was taken. Seemingly dwarfed by its leading coach, No. 50646 busied itself with short railmotor trips in the Bolton area, travelling to Radcliffe and Bradley Fold on the east side of the town. As the signals to the right are 'off', the driver is preparing to enter the coach end driving position customary with this type of working. To the left of the engine's chimney, the expanse of Horwich Works, that they will pass *en route*, can just be determined. Although based at Bolton at the time, No. 50646 was to seek pastures new in the final years of its life, ending up at Bedford until withdrawal in November 1958.

Photo: B.K.B. Green

145. Horwich Works, c.1913. Home at last. Just after 5.30pm in the afternoon and workers make their way out of the main gate on Chorley New Road. This gate was marked 'Loco Works' and was one of three that provided access to and from the site. The third gate was at the east end and served the Foundry, Smithy etc. The second, or middle gate, was adjacent to the canteen. To the left of the gate, just inside, is one of the 'characters' of Horwich Works, a labourer by the name of 'Liverpool Teddy', who held a concession to leave five minutes early and collect newspapers from a local agent to sell to the departing workmen. If sales of the newspaper, *The Bolton Evening News*, were not reaching satisfactory levels, the word 'Special' would be shouted in an effort to drum up interest. The works offices are this side of the water tank, and beyond we come to the location seen in the view below. The site of this gate remained the main entrance right up to the closure of the works. *Photo: National Railway Museum*

146. Horwich Works, 17th July 1907. The locomotive shed at the west end of the works held motive power going into the works as well as those which had received maintenance and were awaiting returning to their respective home depots. One of the roads is occupied by a rail motor. To the left of the shed is the main check lodge while to the right is the bulk of the No.1 erecting shop. *Photo: National Railway Museum*

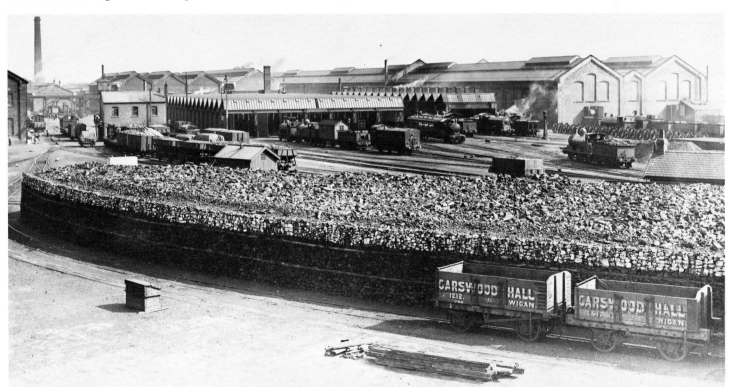

147. Horwich, April 1957. This view of the erecting shop, notwithstanding the type of motive power under construction, had become familiar to generations of workshop employees. It was, however, the last time new locomotives were to be built at the Works. In the left foreground is British Railways Standard Class 4 2-6-0 No. 76089, nearing completion and one of the last batch of 21 locomotives and tenders to be built at Horwich between 14th December 1956 and 27th November 1957. This particular locomotive was allocated to Trafford Park (9E) between May 1957 and December 1961 from whence it was transferred to Bangor. It was withdrawn towards the end of 1966 after giving less than ten years of service. The last locomotive to be built at Horwich was No. 76099 of the same class, bringing to an end a tradition that had begun some sixty eight years earlier with the construction of Lancashire and Yorkshire Railway 2-4-2 Tank locomotive No. 108.

Photo: T.H. Foley

148. Horwich, c.1957/58. Horwich Works was also visited by many an electric railway vehicle. This view in the south bay of the Electric Car Shop shows maintenance in hand on a carriage from the third-rail system in operation around Liverpool and the Wirral. *Photo: T.H. Foley*

149. Horwich Works, c.1903. The railways were very labour intensive and this early view in the north bay of the General Smithy shows the work force responding to the presence of the camera – posing in other words. The bell or bee-hive shaped objects are the hoods to the furnaces whilst to the right of the narrow gauge track is a series of Drop Hammers for forging components. An 18" narrow gauge system in excess of seven miles was built to connect the various parts of the works and required several diminutive locomotives with equally minute names such as *Robin, Wren, Dot, Fly, Wasp* etc., *Wren* incidentally is preserved in the National Railway Museum at York.

Photo: T.H. Foley

150. Horwich, 24th September 1965. Homeward bound workers, some no doubt from the railway offices, await the arrival of the train that will form the 4.51pm to Chorley. Office staff finished earlier than those on the shop floor and it was not unknown for the odd comment to be made about that 'Chorley lot' going early. It was to be the last Friday on the branch, services being withdrawn from the following Monday, there being no Sunday trains. On rising ground behind the station, the buildings of the town are aligned along Chorley Old Road. The station entrance gateway, seen here against the lightened end of the house, was some five hundred yards from the main entrance to Horwich Works. The goods shed and yard have a forlorn look about them, not surprisingly as closure was only a short time away, on 25th April 1966. Rationalization of facilities accelerated the following year when on 29th January, the Horwich Fork was closed, thus eliminating movement from the Bolton direction without reversal. On 3rd March 1967, access to the Horwich Station area was curtailed, buffer stops being erected 30 yards on the station site of the signal box. From the 24th September that year, the lines from Blackrod were re-designated sidings, allowing Loco Junction and Station boxes to be closed.

Photo: P.E. Baughan

151. Horwich, 16th September 1952. L&Y built 2-4-2T, now Class 2P No. 50660, awaits custom with its two coach train to Blackrod. In this motor car age it seems very quaint nowadays that a train should wait to carry people little more than a mile and a half. The service between Horwich and Blackrod/ Bolton was progressively deteriorating and from a 'high' of 1947 with a dozen or so weekday trains each way, 1954 arrived with the loss of evening workings, the service essentially being provided for people travelling to or from work. *Photo: F.W. Shuttleworth*

152. Horwich, 1963. The station signal box was built in 1887, contemporary with the development of the Works. The brick based structure was a design of the Railway Signal Company and contained a 32 lever frame, later replaced by a Lancashire and Yorkshire type. As mentioned above, this box closed on the 24th September 1967.

Photo: G.H. Platt

153. Horwich, 11th April 1961. An attractive view of Horwich Station in its declining years as Stanier 2-6-4T Class 4MT No. 42652 of Bolton Shed waits to depart with a Manchester train. A view inside the goods shed with its crane jib and hook, reflecting upon an age when goods handling was very different from methods used today. There were numerous trains to Manchester via the Fork, the fastest taking 41 minutes for the eighteen mile journey. *Photo: John Marshall*

154. Horwich, 31st March 1964. A train from Manchester Victoria has arrived alongside the platform whilst next to the goods shed an engine and three coaches, the local branch railmotor, awaits its next turn of duty. The single storey station building shows a relationship with others in the area, in particular those on the Bolton to Blackburn line with the full stone chimneys prominent. Above the gable end of the station, it is just possible to distinguish a signal box within the works complex. *Photo: G.J. Biddle*

155. Horwich, August 1937. Another view of the ex-LYR steam railmotor, this time in Horwich station. Numbered 10617, the engine and its trailer were the last of the units to remain in service. This particular photograph shows good end detail, the glazing of course for the Driver's vision when operating from this end. When first built, the end was fully glazed but vestibule corridor connections were added later. (See also plates 22 and 143). *Photo: W. Potter*

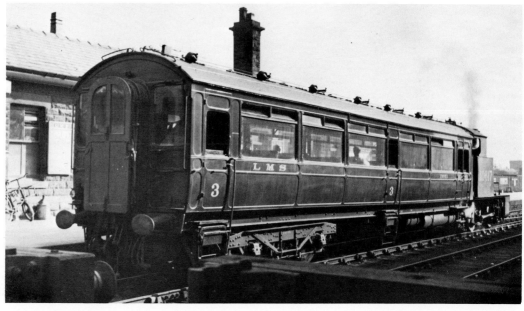

156. Horwich, c.1960. Horwich just made it into the diesel era as this view of Metropolitan-Cammell 2-car DMU illustrates. It has not been possible to establish the reason for this photograph as the units were never regular users of the branch – apart from maintenance visits to the Works – but possibly it was a crew training exercise. The distinctive design of the vehicles has remained familiar since their introduction in the late 1950s. Horwich residents will recognise the outline of the Palace Cinema above the rear of the train and recall periods during wet weather when the soundtrack of the film was effectively drowned by the noise from rain on the corrugated metal roofing.

Photo: Bolton Evening News

157. Horwich Fork, c.1963. In the latter years of the branch, passenger trains using the fork became less frequent. By the spring of 1963, only three weekday workings survived, the 8.13am and 4.54pm to Bolton and the 5.47pm to Manchester Victoria. Saturdays saw a solitary train, which had left Horwich at 12.10pm. The view here shows an unidentified Stanier Class 4 2-6-4T engine with what is possibly the latter of the early evening trains. In the opposite direction, three weekday trains balanced the situation, with arrivals at Horwich being 7.29 (ex-Bolton), 8.52am and 5.29pm (ex-Vic respectively. Although the Fork line closed from the 29th January 1967, the signal box – situated on the main line – continued in use until 14th September 1969. The Loco Junction box, seen here to the right of the white houses, had closed from 24th September 1967, the same day the branch from Blackrod to Horwich had been redesignated as sidings. At this point, the M61 Motorway was to slice through the formation of the Fork line.

Photo: N.R. Knight

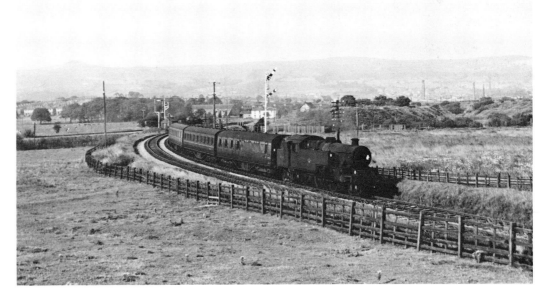

158. Horwich, 25th September 1964. Little need for too much explanation in this view of Horwich on the last day of passenger train workings. A somewhat gloomy scene all round perhaps only lifted by the impressive turnout of the engine, Bolton based Stanier 2-cylinder Class 4 tank engine No 42626. The locomotive had been cleaned in the weeks approaching the event, the band of enthusiasts including photographer and contributor to this book, Steve Leyland. As if observing these rites the engine itself failed a boiler examination two weeks later and ran its own last passenger train on 13th October.

Photo: N.R. Knight

Bolton Great Moor Street

159. Bolton Great Moor Street, c.1936. The triangular pedimented front to Bolton LNWR, or later Great Moor Street, station. It was a more formal, even traditional type of station frontage than Trinity Street but in a less imposing location. The bright posters tend to contrast against the dour, grimy background but if the building had been subjected to the environmental treatment and smokeless air of today, the segmental arches over doorways and windows would show a bright red, blue and white pattern. Note, ironically, the trolley bus wires that provided power to convey passengers by Lancashire United Transport vehicles to Leigh past the front of the station.
Photo: Bolton Evening News

The development of the large city and town stations on a great scale occurred in the last third of the nineteenth century. The first stations were the result of small companies with restricted capital outlay such as the Bolton & Leigh and the Bolton & Manchester whose funds were stretched on surveying, parliamentary approval, land purchases, extensive earthworks and the track itself followed by the locomotives and rolling stock to run on them and to generate business. The station was, after all, a mere stopping place which may, in any case, be developed further by extensions or enlargements of the line, and in terms of expenditure they came bottom of the list.

The early stations tended to have small single storied buildings with just enough to furnish requirements, a booking office and waiting room, particularly for ladies, and a small goods shed with office.

After the piecemeal building of new lines by various small companies the inevitable amalgamation followed to form the large stockholding concerns like the London & North Western Railway and the Lancashire and Yorkshire Railway that ultimately came to dominate Bolton. It was under the ownership of these railways that consolidation took place forming the arterial networks of national commerce.

From 1870 onwards came the great railway age that lasted until 1923. During this period works evolved of immense scale with track patterns of towns and cities looking like the whorls of a thumbprint. Stations were rebuilt into pantheons of classic or gothic architecture with colonnades and vaulting arched roofs, with long sweeping platforms built to accommodate the expanding number of railway users as the companies made themselves more accessible to the public at large. By undertaking mass movement the ticket rates could more

closely match average earnings and thereby encourage the commuter, the holiday and football match trippers, whilst the trains themselves became longer and more accommodating in their facilities. Throughout the thirties, holidays away from home grew in popularity, the Holidays with Pay Act of 1938 meaning that all working people had at least one week of paid holiday.

Bolton featured significantly in all of this for in 1870 it had a population of about 70,000 which was steadily increasing to the point where it vociferously appealed to both companies to improve their amenities and services.

The town's first station was the Bolton & Leigh terminus of 1828 which appears to have consisted of little more that a single building with a few sidings adjoining the Dawes Street side, some likely to be for the use of Hulton Collieries. The goods facilities, sensibly, were situated in the angle between the line to the terminus and the branch to Deansgate warehouse abutting onto Crook Street. The sidings here would also originate from storage roads at the foot of the incline plane. Here, consignments in and out could be marshalled and consequently a gable-roofed goods shed was built. As previously mentioned, this station was given the spectacular coup-de-grace on 28th January 1858, when its 'demolition train' heralded a complete rethink of the site. The 1874 design elevated the station platforms behind an 'Italian' style brick frontage with a descending staircase all of which was suitably imposing for the period. The arched brickwork was segmented in red, blue and white and must have presented a very pleasing addition to the town's architecture. Behind it, four platforms, some three hundred feet long, numbered 1 to 4, provided for the separate routes to Manchester and

EXCHANGE

Reservoir
Ormrod's Mills
(Cotton Spinning & Weaving)

Pin Mill (Cotton Spinning & Weaving)

Reservoir

Royal George Mill (Cotton Spinning)

Engine House

WARD

London & North Western Railway Station

Coal Yard

Weston House

Sovereign Mill (Cotton Spinning)

FLASH STREET

Warehouse (Cotton)

WESTON STREET

REGISTRATION STREET

WESTON COURT

BOLLING STREET

ORMROD STREET

BACK ORMROD STREET

BACK ANDREW STREET

ANDREW STREET

ROWLAND STREET

HALL STREET

SILLABRAND COURT

HEATON ST

Warehouse (Cotton)

WARD STREET

Warehouse (Cotton)

ROYAL ROW

STREET   Ward

Boundary   CROOK   STREET

Parkfield Inn

DAW

Valentine P.H.

The Fairy P.H.

The Red Lion P.H.

Crook Street Warehouse of the London & North Western Railway

The Peacock P.H.

CLOSES   STREET

Cotton Tree P.H.

CARLEY STREET

CHANDOS STREET

Weighing Machine

Warehouse

Reservoir

BOUNDARY STREET

Coal Yard

Coal Yard

Warehouse

Reservoir

B. CARLY STREET

CARLY STREET

MARTIN STREET

Coal Yard

Weighing Machine

Weighing Machine

Warehouse

BRADFORD

London and North Western
Railway (Goods) Station

WARD

Martins Mill (Cotton Spinning & Weaving)

Coal Yard

FLETCHER STREET

Wesleyan Chapel

Salter House

Great Bolton Reservoir No.

Weighing Machine

RIDGMAN

R. C. School
Boys & Girls

Reservoir

Pauls

Liverpool as well as north Wales. The station roof and columns were less individual than the front and repeated the LNWR overall roof style with glazed endscreens and multistrands of tie-rods. The adjoining sidings of Hulton's Collieries were arranged alongside and located above coal drops. Crook Street of course had to be bridged and in later years the road beneath was recessed to allow clearance for tram cars. New plans for the goods yard were drawn up in 1862 allowing for fifteen sidings and a three storeyed warehouse. Furthermore, in 1900, the LNWR purchased and converted the Victoria Mill Building – later known as Bridgeman Street Warehouse – on the eastern side of the line. Added to this was a new shed for storing machinery. In the yard itself was built a fruit and vegetable warehouse which backed onto Chandos Street.

Sidings occupiers in the locality were as follows: J. Briggs and Son, Hick Hargreaves (Soho Ironworks), Bridgeman Street Siding, Walmsleys Atlas Forge Ironworks, W. Townson, Higher Swan Lane, J. Booth and Co at Fletcher Street and J. Booth and Co Hulton Siding. Magee Marshall & Co, Bolton Co-op Coal Yard, T.D. Roscoe & Co Ltd, LAC Bridgewater Colliery, Bolton Corporation Bus Garage.

It is not clear where engine servicing took place during the early years of the line but with the opening of the branch from Tyldesley to Bolton, which was integrated into the new station structure, and the extensive services over the Liverpool route, engine facilities were brought into line with the new works and a steam shed opened at Plodder Lane in 1875. A four road shed of 'northlight' pattern, it was later extended by another building with six roads in 1890. The first engines there would likely be Webb 2-4-2 5ft 6ins tanks supplemented with 0-6-2 'Coal' tanks for working the Kenyon Junction side of the service. The Manchester trains were worked from Exchange station with engines from Patricroft, of which Plodder Lane was a sub shed. Bolton LNWR saw many of the Webb eight-coupled engines that were diagrammed from Patricroft and Wigan Springs Branch for the working of the goods trains, in particular Hulton Collieries traffic provided some hard work for locomotives over the notorious gradients of the ex-Bolton & Leigh line.

On 1st April, 1875, the LNWR operated through carriages from Bolton to Euston via Manchester Exchange which would neatly avoid the discordant gap between the L&Y at Victoria and the LNWR (London Road) for intending London-bound Boltonians.

A coveted duty for Plodder Lane men who were largely restricted to local work was to have a Patricroft 'Precursor' 4-4-0 on a Chester job during the summer. In LMS days the ex-LYR 2-4-2 tanks would appear on workings into Great Moor Street from Manchester. With the formation of British Railways the Ivatt and Standard type 2-6-2 tank engines were rostered from Plodder Lane and it was these engines that operated the last passenger services in 1954. In 1942, as part of a wartime emergency, the passenger service into Great Moor Street was temporarily suspended. ·

Although there is not a fair comparison of volume traffic the LNWR station presented greater architectural features to the Bolton skyline than did the LYR, which was a lugubriously perched block of fierce Accrington brick made worse by a gaunt and clumsy canopy which would hardly appropriate the refined term of 'port cochere'. That being said, space was obviously its prime virtue, followed by longevity, for in 1954 the ex-LNWR station that had from 1923 been know as Bolton (Great Moor Street), for with the formation of the LMS in that year both stations came under the same ownership which, in keeping with hundreds of others required a distinction to be made, was proposed for closure.

Bolton no longer needed two routes to Manchester and Liverpool and the station closed from 29th March 1954. As there were no Sunday services this effectively meant Saturday 27th March. Closing along with it on the Manchester line were Plodder Lane, Little Hulton and Walkden (Low Level). On the Kenyon Junction Line, Atherton (Bag Lane), Atherleigh, West Leigh and Pennington. Rumworth and Daubhill and Chequerbent had been closed on 3rd March 1952. At the time of closure the station was handling 26 trains each weekday with 360 passengers, whereas fifty years earlier it had been 75 trains a day. The last train from Bolton to Kenyon Junction was a two-coach push-pull working with a BR standard 2-6-2 tank No. 84003, whilst the final train to Manchester was dutifully drawn by the much more favoured Stanier 2-6-4 tank No. 42574.

These were not quite the last vapours of coal and steam from passenger trains in the station, for each year of Bolton's annual holiday week in late June the rival Trinity Street station found itself unable to cope, Great Moor Street handling the north Wales holiday traffic up

until 1959. On a personal note the author remembers climbing those dark damp stairs to chilly platforms and boarding a train for Prestatyn. Even in the heat of June, there was a distinctly disinterred feel to the place. However, viewing Crook Street from on high was an appealing novelty and winding through an unfamiliar section of Bolton's industrial heartland was not without pathos. Freight traffic continued on the line until 17th June 1963, when the section from Howe Bridge North Junction to Pennington Junction was closed. The coal drops alongside the passenger train shed were used until 1964.

On 7th April 1964 the contracting firm of T.W. Ward of Sheffield started to take up track in the station. This was loaded into three empty coal wagons and shunted into the middle road. The track, chairs and sleepers were hauled away by ex-LMS tank No. 47378. The two remaining coal sidings continued to be visited daily by the 'Jinty' that would exchange about 6 wagons. This constituted the last diagrammed working into the station.

On 11th May 1964, what remained of the sidings of the original line to Daubhill were closed down. Crook Street yard itself continued until 26th April 1965, although it continued as a private siding for the NCB until October 1967. The last part of the B & L to be in use was from Hulton's Sidings down to Chequerbent Bank and Howe East and West Junctions which were closed on 6th January 1969.

The road bridge over Crook Street was removed in December 1966 and the station structure was demolished at about the same time. The elevated track bed was used as a car park until 1974 when the entire site was levelled.

160. Bolton Great Moor Street, 24th September 1965. Few Bolton residents will remember the station in the pristine condition seen in the view in the front of the book. The building remained for a number of years after closure in the deteriorating condition to be found in this view from the corner of Black Horse Street, only the advertisers appearing to be interested in the site.
Photo: P.E. Baughan

161. Bolton Great Moor Street. A view little changed from the days of its opening in 1875. The roof appears to be its original length and typifies LNWR design and construction methods of the period. The station staff are on platform one which would have been for Kenyon Junction departures/arrivals, along with platform two. Manchester trains were served the other side of the island platform on three and four. Note the hanging gas lamps with lantern heads half blacked out in line with wartime regulations.
Photo: Bolton Evening News

162. Bolton Great Moor Street, 27th December 1952. BR built Ivatt tank No. 41215 prepares to leave with the 1.20pm train to Manchester Exchange. This was a Saturdays Only working which filled the otherwise four hour gap in the timetable. It is not clear when the overall roof was cut back but it was an economy subjected to many similar buildings throughout the railway network. This 2-6-2T locomotive was built at Crewe in 1948 to an LMS design and was one of a small batch allocated to Plodder Lane.
Photo: N.R. Knight

163. Bolton Great Moor Street, 4th April 1959. The Railway Correspondence and Travel Society (RCTS) South Lancashire Tour is seen here on the part of its itinerary which included this visit to former LNWR territory. Commencing at Manchester Victoria (1.5pm), the special train had run via Radcliffe to Bolton Trinity Street before taking in the Halliwell branch on its way to Horwich. The 'return' journey started by negotiating Adlington Junction and the Whelley Loop before heading for Bolton Great Moor Street via Howe Bridge West Junction. Following reversal, the train travelled via Little Hulton and Eccles to the Weaste Wharf of the Manchester Ship Canal. It was intended that the tour should end at Manchester Exchange around 5.21pm, the cost a princely 12s 6d.

Photo: Peter Ward

164. Bolton Great Moor Street, 4th April 1959. Engine to the RCTS Tour train, 2-4-2T No. 50644, has taken time off to replenish her tanks. Note the detail around the column – brazier, lamp, etc. This former L&Y locomotive was based at Dallam (Warrington) during the last years of her life and was actually withdrawn some seven months after this event. Although regular passenger services had been withdrawn some five years previously, Great Moor Street station still had a neat and tidy appearance about it.

Photo: Peter Ward

165. Bolton Great Moor Street, 4th April 1959. A most unusual view of the station for which we are indebted to the photographer for climbing the bracket signal seen above. The panorama takes in, to the left, the water tank for the station whilst to the right of the parked carriage is the gable end of the Sweet Green Tavern in Crook Street. The background is filled by the large complex of Soho Foundry, founded by Benjamin Hick, whose early associations with the railways, first the Bolton & Leigh, and then the LNWR, are well documented. The station signal box can be seen beyond the train and was built for the opening of the new station in 1874. By the time of the photograph, its status had been reduced to that of a ground frame, although still with its 'Bolton No. 1' nameboards on front and ends. It was finally taken out of use from 1st October 1967. The taller structure to the right was part of the boiler/engine house building which supplied power for Crook Street Goods warehouse.

Photo: Peter Ward

166. Bolton Great Moor Street, 12th April 1962. A silent and melancholy prospect of Great Moor Street station awaiting its fate. This view from the steps of the signal box shows the girders of Crook Street bridge (No. 38) and the station from a vantage point rarely available to the public. The extent to which the platforms were once covered can be determined. Signal arms have been recovered and only the one time Hulton's Coal Siding, by now National Coal Board, to the right of the picture, shows any sign of business. The dullness of the picture is not intended, the weather was equally dismal. *Photo: John Marshall*

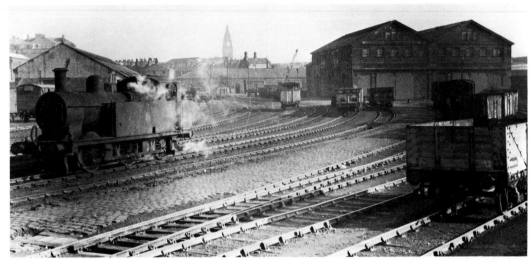

167. Crook Street Goods, 12th April 1962. Crook Street goods yard had two extensive warehouses, Chandos Street to the left, the main Crook Street warehouse to the right. Across the back of the site, against Crook Street, were the stables. This view shows Patricroft 'Jinty' Class 3F 0-6-0T No. 47430 busying itself amongst the wagons. It was all to end on 26th April 1965 when the depot was closed to all but private sidings. From that date, merchandise accounting for less than a wagon load or that requiring cranage was to be dealt with at Manchester Road. Other traffic was transferred to Halliwell. The list of private sidings was formidable:- Bolton Co-op Society, J. Briggs & Sons, Hick Hargreaves Ltd., Magee Marshall Ltd., N.C.B. Crook Street, N.C.B. Dawes Street, W. Townson & Sons, T. Walmsley & Sons, Stones Hutchinson, GPO. Following closure of the Roe Green Junction–Little Hulton Junction section in 1961, Crook Street was served from the Atherton line, a situation lasting until 15th February 1968 when the Hultons Siding to Fletcher Street section was closed. Townsons Siding ground frame also closed on the same day. The site seen here was purchased by Hick Hargreaves in 1967. *Photo: John Marshall*

168. Crook Street, 16th March 1918. The view here shows a spectacular conclusion to the journey of LNWR 0-6-0 saddle tank from the colliery sidings at Little Hulton. This late night escapade occurred between the hours of 11 and 12 when the engine brake power proved insufficient to control the loaded wagons as the train descended towards Bolton. Realising their predicament, the driver and fireman jumped clear of the engine as it was diverted as a runaway into Crook Street Yard. The slight reversal of gradient did nothing to improve the situation and the train careered towards the buffers. Demolishing this unfortunate obstacle, it continued across the yard on the cobbles, smashing through the boundary wall into Crook Street before entering one of the terraced houses and dropping into the cellar. Amazingly, no one was injured, but the reaction of any sleeping residents in the rooms above defies imagination. *Photo: LNWR Society*

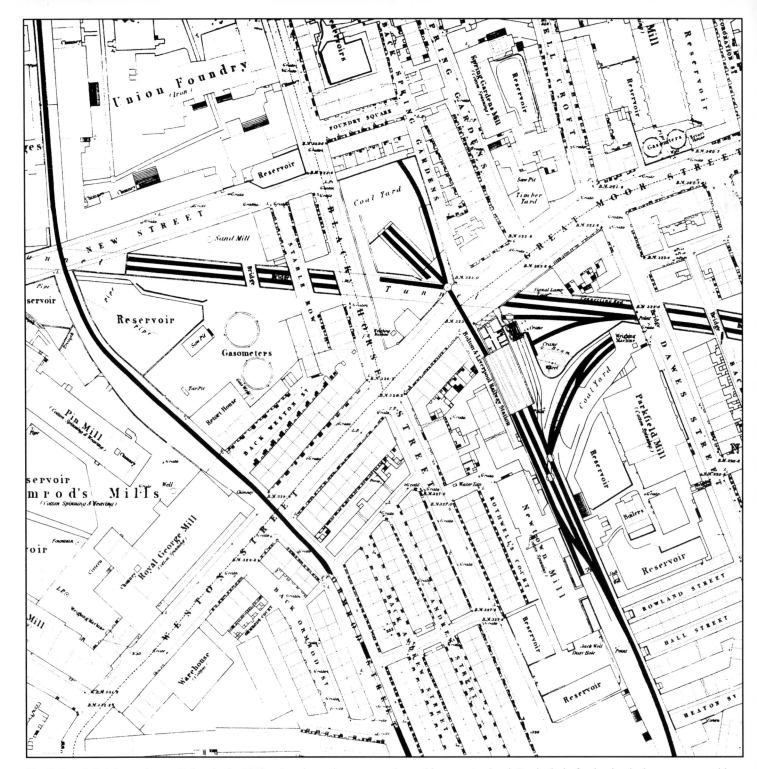

The Bolton & Leigh terminus at Bolton in the 1850s when the station was not elevated but at street level. Particularly fascinating is the wagon turntable at the end of Hulton's Sidings (coal yard) on the right of the station which by means of another siding actually connects this line with the Bolton & Preston and Liverpool lines. Of interest also are the sidings and coal yard facing the station across Great Moor Street, whilst from Crook Street the long branch snakes its way along Ormrod and other streets to reach the foundry of Rothwell, Hick (Union Foundry). It is perhaps worth noting that between 8.00am and 8.30am each morning, all road traffic would have to pause to allow wagons to be exchanged between the foundry and the yard. The railway warehouse that was the terminus of this branch on White Lion Brow was enlarged in 1880.   *Bolton Library Archives*

Below: Extract from Bradshaw 19th October 1839

BOLTON AND LEIGH RAILWAY.

To Liverpool and Manchester

Quarter past Seven . . . . Second Class Train	Half past Two . . . . Second Class Train
Twenty minutes before Nine First ditto	Quarter past Five . . . . Second ditto
Ten minutes before Eleven . . First ditto	

To Wigan and Preston--Quarter past 7; Twenty minutes before 9; Ten minutes before 11; and Half-past Two.

To St. Helens, by all the Second Class Trains | **To Runcorn Gap,** Quarter past 7, & Quarter past 5.

ON SUNDAYS, TO ALL THE ABOVE NAMED PLACES.—Quarter before 7, a.m. and Quarter past 5, p.m. 2nd Class Trains.

Fares--FIRST CLASS--To Liverpool 5s. 6d., Manchester 2s. 6d., Preston 6s., Wigan 3s., St. Helens 4s. 6d., Runcorn Gap 4s.

SECOND CLASS--Liverpool 4s., Manchester 2s., Preston 4s., Wigan, 2s. 6d., St. Helens 3s. 6d., Runcorn Gap 3s.

169. Plodder Lane, 13th April 1955.
The shed as seen just after closure was actually an addition to the depot built in 1874. The original four road shed, situated to the left of the structure seen here soon became crowded, resulting in a six road extension completed in the 1890s. The goods shed serving Plodder Lane can be seen to the left and was situated on the far side of the line to Roe Green. It was somewhat large for a 'local' station and could be approached from both directions, being controlled from Plodder Lane's two signal boxes. Goods facilities were withdrawn from 30th January 1965 although a limited amount of coal trading continued. From 7th May 1961, the line south of Little Hulton Junction was closed, the remaining stretch from Lever Street, Bolton, being designated sidings. The signal boxes at Plodder Lane and at Little Hulton Junction became ground frames.
Photo: F.W. Shuttleworth

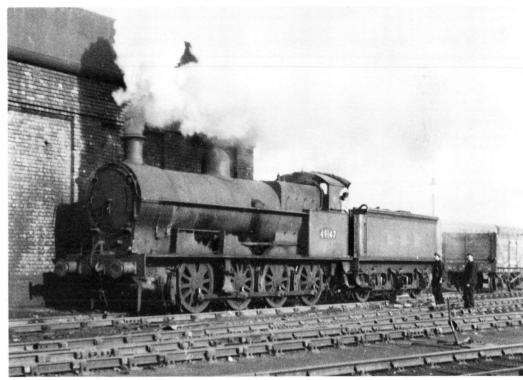

170. Plodder Lane, 24th April 1951.
Carrying out some form of duty in the depot alongside the coaling stage is one of Plodder Lane's (10D) own engines, ex-LNWR 0-8-0 No. 49147. Following closure of the depot, the locomotive was transferred to Patricroft where she worked out her days, being withdrawn in September 1962.
Photo: R.M. Casserley

171. Plodder Lane, April 1939.
Another former LNWR locomotive sits outside the depot, this particular example, LMS No. 27645 being fitted for auto-train working. The engines were popularly known as 'Coal Tanks' and were built to a design introduced in 1892 by Mr. F.W. Webb at Crewe. Examples remained at Plodder Lane until 1949 when, in one fell swoop, they were replaced by a batch of Ivatt 2-6-2 tank engines.
Photo: W. Potter

172. Plodder Lane, 1949. Replacements for the motive power discussed in the previous caption are seen here although they too were displaced after a relatively short period by British Railways Standard Class 2-6-2Ts. Ivatt 2-6-2T No. 41213 seen here, wandered somewhat throughout her life, taking in Walsall and Warrington prior to a brief spell at Barnstaple which preceded withdrawal. No. 41215 enjoyed a more parochial existence, working out of Chester until December 1959 before a transfer to Lancaster where after six years of service, she too was withdrawn.
Photo: B.K.B. Green

173. Plodder Lane, 24th April 1951. Ivatt 2-6-2T No. 41211 hauls its train up the 1 in 137 gradient towards Plodder Lane Station on its way to Manchester Exchange. The signal box beyond the rear of the train is Plodder Lane No. 2 which controlled access to/from the engine shed. The first carriage behind the engine is a former L&YR type whilst the third vehicle was LNWR built for Stockport District sets.
Photo: R.M. Casserley

174. Plodder Lane, 27th March 1954. On the last Saturday before closure BR Standard Class 2MT 2-6-2T No. 84001 waits in the station with the 1.20 (SO) Bolton Great Moor Street to Manchester Exchange train. The thirty seven minute journey, calling also at Little Hulton, Walden Low Level, Worsley, Monton Green, Eccles, Seedley, Cross Lane and Ordsall Lane, compared favourably with the more direct Trinity Street – Manchester Victoria service. Visible beyond the bridge is a surviving LNWR semaphore signal.
Photo: N.R. Knight

175. Little Hulton, 27th March 1954. Further down the line, the 1.20pm has once again become the target of a photographer. Little Hulton Station was located in a cutting on the north side of Manchester Road East (A6). Tramways and later, buses, provided intense competition, no doubt contributing towards the demise of the train service. The station did not have any goods facilities but provided generous waiting accommodation on each of the platforms which were connected by a footbridge to the booking office at road level.

Photo: R.H. Hughes

176. Walkden Yard, 15th June 1952. A little over midway between Little Hulton and Walkden Low Level stations, Walkden Sidings provided an exchange point at which traffic was able to enter and leave the railway system of the Bridgewater Collieries, a network which literally criss-crossed the area. The collieries line, which linked Mosley Common and Ashton Field pits crossed the LNW a quarter of a mile on the Bolton side of Walkden Station. Walkden area workshops are seen here with a cluster of saddle tank engines between duties. The winding gear to Ellesmere's two pits is seen in the upper right of the picture. Bridgewater Collieries had become part of Manchester Collieries Ltd., in 1929, nationalization taking place under the umbrella of the National Coal Board on 1st January 1947. *Photo: N.R. Knight*

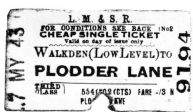

177. Walkden Low Level, n.d. A perfect example of the LNWR trains in the Bolton area where that company is usually seen as being overshadowed by the Lancashire and Yorkshire Railway. This Webb 2-4-2 tank is at Walkden LNWR or, as it became – Low Level – in June 1924. The engine is lined black but the scene is relieved by the distinctive livery, carmine and ermine white, of the coaches. This view towards Manchester has Walkden Road – now the A575 – crossing the background. Brindley Street runs from left to right at the top of the embankment, the Ellesmere Hotel dominating the junction with the main road.

Photo: courtesy Frank Mullineux

178. Daubhill, 22nd July 1963. A seemingly mundane but interesting duty for Patricroft based 8F No. 48178 as it traverses a siding that could claim to be the oldest piece of railway in Lancashire, on the Bolton and Leigh line, site of the original Daubhill station. The engine is alongside Sunnyside Mills, not far from the coal sidings in Adelaide Street; where the old route was truncated in 1885.

Photo: John Marshall

179. Daubhill, 22nd July 1963. A scene which became increasingly frustrating to road users was the level crossing in St. Helens Road adjacent to the Stags Head public house. By this time, the movements were made somewhat surreptitiously early on a Sunday morning. This 7am view shows No. 48178 hauling empty wagons back towards Daubhill junction. Instructions for crossing St. Helens Road were quite specific *'Engines travelling to or from the LMS Daubhill goods lines must not foul the St. Helens roadway without permission of the LMS gateman. Guards and others to assist the gateman to properly protect the crossing':* LMS Sectional Appendix 1.1.1931. *Photo: John Marshall*

180. Daubhill Junction, 28th June 1963. After returning from the Sunnyside Mills siding via the coal yard, No. 48178 waits at the junction with its short train of empty wagons. The original Bolton & Leigh line can be seen climbing away beneath the bridge carrying Deane Church Lane. The signal box lost its block post status from 10th May 1965, but continued as a ground frame. The line between Bolton Fletcher Street and Hultons Sidings was completely closed from 15th February 1968. *Photo: John Marshall*

181. Chequerbent Incline, n.d. An explicit view showing the undulating 1 in 30 gradient that ascended from the town of Atherton. The Ivatt 2-6-2 tank attacks the climb in earnest with its ex-LNWR pull-push unit providing an interesting period piece. Train services between Manchester and Bolton via Tyldesley had ended on the 4th May 1942.

182. Chequerbent, 31st May 1968. Stanier 8F No. 48327; a Patricroft engine, received a much needed push from sister locomotive No. 48529, recently transferred to Newton Heath from Edge Hill. The train of limestone filled hopper wagons would be on its way to the quarries near Hultons Siding, the line beyond here having been closed some three months earlier. It was indeed a period of 'endings', as both locomotives were to be withdrawn in June and the section of line seen here between Howe Bridge East Junction and Hultons Sidings was to go on 21st January 1969. To the right of the picture are the partially overgrown spoil heaps of Pretoria Colliery. The train had originated in the Buxton area, train crews from there having brought the working to Atherton where it was split prior to being taken forward in shorter, and lighter, units due to difficulties with the gradient. *Photo: N.R. Knight*

183. Chequerbent Bank, n.d. An early view of the signal box built towards the top end of the 1 in 30 gradient, in fact if one takes the perspective into account, it appears almost possible to perceive the severity of the gradient against the horizontal brickwork joints. The box was a composite – brick and timber – structure. It has not been possible to establish when it closed but it certainly appeared in the 1931 Sectional Appendix. *Photo: Heydey Publishing Co*

184. Westhoughton: Pretoria Colliery, December 1910. A very emotional photograph, taken at the Colliery at the time of the disaster of the 21st December 1910, when 344 miners were killed following a gas explosion. Few words are needed other than to say that the photograph is thought to have been taken as the Salvation Army conducted a prayer meeting whilst bodies were being recovered. It is quite possible that the scale of the disaster was not fully known at this time. The look of incomprehension is visible on every face, with Westhoughton, barely more than a village at the time, bearing the brunt of the tragedy. The last of the coal mines in the Westhoughton area closed in 1935 as a result of flooding. *Photo: Hulton Picture Library*

185. Hulton Colliery, Chequerbent n.d. An interesting photograph from the railway point of view. Groups of Hulton's private owner wagons lined up beneath the coal drops. Evidently, tubs brought from below would run along the timber staging located above and at right angles to the wagons and have their loads tipped directly into the vehicles beneath. One coal drop point appears to be inside the shelter above the pair of wagons in the left foreground. Note the brick built engine house behind the winding derrick, equipment that would power the rise and fall of cages.

Photo: Westhoughton Library

186. Atherton Bag Lane, 27th March 1954. Bolton bound with the 4.29pm train from Kenyon Junction, British Railways Standard Class 2 2-6-2T No. 84004 pauses at Atherton Bag Lane (4.43pm) on the last day of passenger working over the line. Due in Bolton Great Moor Street at 4.55pm this push-pull, or Rail Motor working, had started its journey as the 4.23 from Newton-le-Willows. Upon leaving Atherton, the train would soon encounter the steeply graded Chequerbent Bank, although the need for the driver to ease off at the top had receded with the closure of Chequerbent station on the 3rd March 1952, same day as the fate befell Rumworth & Daubhill. Although a station at Atherton had existed in those far off Bolton & Leigh days, the design of the buildings dated from the later Victorian period. The somewhat heavy canopies, although of LNWR vintage, had more than a passing resemblance to Lancashire and Yorkshire Railway design. The signal box continued in use until 21st January 1969 when the remaining lines in use between Tyldesley, Howe Bridge East Junction, and Hultons Sidings were closed.
Photo: N.R. Knight

187. Atherton Bag Lane, 15th June 1963. The 'Bag Lane' suffix was added on 2nd June 1924 to distinguish it from its L&Y neighbour, which became Central. In the weeks before withdrawal of goods facilities 'Austerity' 2-8-0 No. 90440, a Wigan Springs Branch (8F) engine, idles its time in the sidings. The goods yard was closed for public use from 7th October 1963, whereas the engine had been withdrawn in September and stored at Bolton prior to being sent to Horwich for scrapping. *Photo: John Marshall*

188. Pennington South Junction, 27th March 1954. Between last day passenger workings on the Bolton–Kenyon Junction line, the photographer captured ex-LNWR 0-8-0 No. 49149 hauling a train of loaded coal wagons, possibly from nearby Bickershaw Colliery. The Eccles, Tyldesley and Wigan line runs across the background. Some six years later, this West to South 'chord' line had been relegated to siding status, albeit retaining through running facilities. This connection was designated temporary from 29th November 1964. However, Pennington South Junction signal box closed from 14th March 1966, making the previous arrangement redundant.
Photo: B.K.B. Green

Above and Left: Extract from a 1909 edition of Bradshaw give details of the LNWR services between Manchester (Exchange) and Bolton (Great Moor Street), and the alternative route avoiding Bolton to Wigan and Blackpool. The smaller table reveals the fact of a through coach facility between Bolton LNWR (Great Moor Street), along the Ordsall Lane Branch, and Euston.

189. Pennington, 27th March 1954. Pennington was situated on a level stretch of line just over a mile from Kenyon Junction, a mere four minutes away. In the distance, the line climbs to a point where it is crossed by the East Lancs Road, a vantage point from which even today, the disused formation cuts a dominant furrow which has stood the test of time. Another last day view shows No. 84004 on its return journey from Bolton. *Photo: B.K.B. Green*

Kenyon Junction

Kenyon Junction can lay claim to being one of the earliest of what became a British institution, the country junction station, when in 1831, the Kenyon and Leigh Junction Railway opened to provide a connection between the Bolton and Leigh and Liverpool and Manchester Railways. Although not a Bolton area station, its affinity with the town remained throughout its life by virtue of the service which ran between the two points. The two photographs (190 and 191) illustrate the pride which the staff had for their station, reflected in the award of 1st Prize in the 1947 Liverpool District Competition for the Best Kept Station.

190. Station staff, with others, from left to right are as follows: Arthur Smith (*Clerk*), Fred Taylor (*Porter*), P.J. Fisher, E.J. Jarman (*Station Master*), J.C. Byrom (*Passenger Manager*), Walter Ainsworth (*Relief Porter*), James Dawson (*Junior Porter*).

191. The station staff once again pose for the photographer, an example of their handiwork to the right of the picture. It has not been possible to identify all those in this view. However, the end pair to the left are Maurice Belshaw and Fred Taylor. Arthur Smith, who wisely kept the photographs in safe keeping, is fourth from left. Station Master Jarman stands with the unidentified trio whilst Grade 2 Porter Les MacFarlane holds the notice board that heralds their achievement.

Photos: Courtesy Arthur Smith

192. **Kenyon Junction, c.1959.** Patricroft based 'Jubilee' 4-6-0 No. 45645 *Collingwood*, races through the empty main line platforms of Kenyon Junction with a Liverpool bound express, possibly from Newcastle. The station was within a couple of years of closure but still enjoyed a train service which reflected better days. Westbound trains emanated from Manchester Exchange, the majority travelling via Tyldesley and calling at stations whose names are now consigned to the history books, namely Cross Lane, Monton Green, Worsley, Ellenbrook, and Leigh. Bolton trains, until withdrawal in 1954, used the platforms to the left of the picture. The station lost its remaining passenger services from the 2nd January 1961. Goods facilities were withdrawn on 1st August 1963 but private sidings remained for a short time to cater for coal traffic. Kenyon finally lost its junction status on 11th May 1969 when the route from Eccles Junction via Tyldesley was taken out of use. The main line still remains of course but mother nature has since virtually obliterated all trace of this once sizeable station. *Photo: T. Lewis.*

BOLTON ENGINEMEN

193. Driver Joe McCloughlan and Passed Cleaner Malcolm Frost on a Bury 'Crab' at Bury shed in 1958 prior to going up to Haslingden on a shunting turn. *Photo: courtesy Malcolm Frost*

During the compilation of this book I had the fortunate and happy opportunity of meeting the men who worked on the railways of Bolton up to and in some cases after the age of steam. To say this was a rewarding experience would be an understatement but it should not have been surprising for I have never met a group of such good working companions. The *bonhomie* at Bolton must have been second to none, a situation often found amongst men having to work in arduous and often dangerous situations, not to mention uncomfortable. Like the countless mill operatives and large scale heavy industry workers, it is an age consigned to Bolton's history. The following anecdotes, told by the men themselves are a contribution to that history and a section of the working people that played their part in it.

JOHN MATHER.
John Mather served all his railway working life from 1934 to 1975, at Bolton shed, save for a brief period of four months at Carnforth. First of all as a knocker-up (raising weary enginemen from their beds by all means possible) and then as a 'bar' lad, a particularly grimy and levelling experience for any would be engineman, of cleaning out fireboxes. He finally became a 'passed cleaner' in 1937, which meant that he was at last riding the footplate and doing firing turns before becoming a fully fledged fireman in 1942 and a driver in 1946.

'My father started at Plodder Lane depot. Do you know, he used to go out at Monday and she never saw him again until the following Sunday. That was a practice on the LNWR you know. He used to go out with a train, especially if he went to one of those main line depots, and he would book off and go to a hostel. Following morning he would report for work and they would enquire of him if he knew the road and if he did, that would be another journey that could be taking him further and further away from home, all the time booking off and booking on. He told me that the closest he could get to travel home was Wigan, the main line, and he booked off and walked it home, some nine miles. He knew the road as far south as Rugby and north to Carlisle.

I once went on Horwich holidays and had a Midland class 4 to work an excursion to Blackpool. I played heck because I was given an engine to work a train that had just come off Horwich works and not had trials. I could tell this because they always put a plate on the step that said *experiment*, which meant not surprisingly that something on the loco was experimental. I didn't know what, but to chance it on a heavily loaded passenger train was putting a big responsibility onto the driver. As it turned out the thing that was experimental on this one was the eccentrics. Normally, all the bearings were white metal. Well on this occasion they experimented for cheapness with cast iron. We left Horwich from the branch and got out onto the main line at Blackrod hauling the coaches. I had only gone a quarter of a mile when the engine started to shake and go backwards and forwards, running about four or five yards then coming back. My mate said, 'Heck! whats wrong with it?', I replied, 'I've a good idea'. So I says 'Jus' get on the framing and have a look in the motion'. He comes back and says, 'Hell fire, you want to go and have a look in there'. 'Why, what's wrong with her?' So I went to look, and the eccentrics – there were two eccentrics for each side, the top one being for foregear and the bottom one for back gear and on the left-hand side. The rods were made of malleable steel, and the force had simply pulled the rod out and just

gone underneath. The eccentric strap had burst and what had happened was that these cast iron linings had overheated, swelled and siezed to clamp on the journal, tying the rods up like strands of spaghetti.

So I says to him, 'You had better get back to the box and put detonators down, and I'll walk it to the next one, whichever is the nearest and ring control for another engine to come and pull me off'. I also requested a fitter. Well, the relieving engine had to come from Bolton and in the end they pushed me back on the branch and an inspector came and said, 'Whats up with this thing?', so I told him. He had a look and said, 'Well what a daft thing to do'. What transpired was that they had been carrying out this experiment and we would test the engines running light before sending them off to their respective sheds where they inevitably failed when running with a train. Now this particular inspector was pleased that it had happened this way – by putting a modified engine straight onto a train – and so the running department would be able to get this practice terminated.

On one occasion Newton Heath were short of men and they asked me if I would fill in on my rest day. Me and my mate were therefore sent to Newton Heath to work a relief train. The whole point was that my engine would be ready to go off shed when I got there. It was the 8.45am Manchester to Blackpool. We then had to work another train back from Blackpool at 2 o'clock, Salford first stop, with the same engine.
When we get to the shed we find our engine is No. 5635 *Tobago*, a 3-cylinder Jubilee. My mate was dead chuffed, 'Not often we get one of these', he says, quite beaming he was. But it wouldn't be long before the smile would leave 'is face very rapidly.

Now this driver and fireman when they saw us coming said, 'Its alright mate, its ready for going'. I noticed that the firebox door was closed and we had fifteen minutes to get off the depot so off we go into Lightbowne Sidings. The Guard comes and says, curiously, '5635 – it rings a bell, this'. He starts flicking through his note book but couldn't find what he was looking for and he just looks up after a short time and says, 'It must be something and nothing'.

So off we go into Manchester and couples up, with Bolton first stop. Do you know, that lad firing had sweat rolling out of him for he put his injector on leaving Manchester and never closed it so that when we got into Bolton we just had enough [water] covering the bottom nut. Footplate inspector comes up and I says to him, 'look at this lot, its ridiculous'. All he could say was, 'Well you'll just have to manage with it'. I turns to my mate and says, 'Just keep at it, you'll have to keep at it, there is something definitely wrong here with just using water continuously'.

Anyway after what must have been one of the most gruelling runs ever for my mate, we finally managed to get the train into Blackpool and he was just like a wet rag. The train was taken away from us and we went onto the depot to turn. While he's turning I pulls smoke plate out of firebox and have a look. Six superheater tubes pouring with water, the fire was out at the front!

So *Tobago* didn't go back with us, thank God. After an inspection by a boiler smith at Blackpool, who was appalled, it was ignominiously dragged to Crewe.

MR. T. SIBBERING.
'Just after the war we used to work the last train out of Victoria to Horwich before working back and finishing at Bolton. We often left the coaches at Horwich, running round and pushing them up to the stops so they were ready for the first train out in the morning. One night we were doing this there was a sailor on the platform, kit bag on his shoulder and looking a bit bewildered. He says to us, 'Wer's docks?' We both looked at him a bit puzzled and said, 'What docks?' Mind you, it was well after ten at night and what had transpired was that he thought he had caught the train to Harwich at Manchester whereupon we enlightened him that this was Horwich! 'Anyway, the best we could do for him was to take him on the footplate back to Bolton'.

JOE STRICKLETON.
We used to go to Ancoats with the Carlisle train with class 9's and I fired for one driver who needed his own colliery! I didn't use a normal firing shovel with these particular engines, I used a labouring coal baggers shovel. They had a shallow firebox you know, the 9's so I used to take the smoke plate out and fill it up as much as I could when we were leaving Bolton. We used to have a bank engine from Bradshawgate up to Sough tunnel, by which time I had put a ton in the box, and by gum, this feller could use coal. At Bolton we had railmotors, Lancashire & Yorkshire tanks, L&Y A classes, three 'Austin 7's', class 4 tanks and we would have at least 5 to 8 engines all the time being broken in for Horwich Works. 'Teddy Bears', 'Crabs', and little class 3 taper boiler tanks. The 'Teddy Bears' didn't last long after 1944, about 1950 I think they went. Wigan was the last place to have them and they had a smaller version called 'Sea Pigs', a class 6.

The longest turn that I ever heard of for a freight train was from Birmingham to Carlisle with one set of men. That was an afternoon job done by Saltley men and went via Derby, Sheffield, Leeds, Skipton, Hellifield and Carlisle.

I've been to Astley bridge with No. 11348, a little Lanky engine saddle tank, they called it the Halliwell Pilot. You could put a piece of wood between the bunker and underneath the reversing lever – which only needed six turns backwards and forwards – and with the short hand brake, you could sit there all day shunting backwards and forwards, they were lovely little engines for that.

Just near to St.Peter's Way was a place called Craddock Lane where we used to refill with water when we were on banking duty. At Craddock Lane Sidings there were sometimes three banking engines. Of the trains that were banked from Bolton, Rochdale to Hellifield was the first, about 6.30 or 7 o'clock in the morning. Then Brindle Heath–Carlisle, 9.56; Ancoats to Carlisle, Bolton to Colne, 11.30; Heaton Mersey to Hellifield, Brindle Heath to Blackburn, Kearsley to Blackburn (this was coal), Halliwell Pilot. Engines used on Bolton to Colne parcels were 2322, 2332, 2352, 2379.

Lanky class A tanks had lifting injectors on the floor that used to get warm when the water got warm in summer and if that happened you had to rub the feedpipe with cotton waste soaked in cold water.

Trains that used to work over the north side of the Bolton West triangle were the Bullfield to Halliwell and Bamfurlong to Halliwell, Westhoughton to Blackburn, all freight trains. The only passenger workings that ever went over there were excursion trains, and empty stock for Horwich carriage sidings.

194. Still mates on the footplate – Malcolm Frost and Joe Strickleton on the East Lancashire Railway at Bury in July 1987.

Photo: Courtesy Malcolm Frost

At Great Moor Street they only had one what you would call a main line job and that was to Edge Hill. For this they would use a Derby 4F or a Super D. Their only passenger work was push-pulls around Warrington and as far as Widnes but mainly to Kenyon Junction and Manchester Exchange. They also had a night goods job to Warrington. In the fifties, Plodder Lane had five Derby 4F's, a couple of Jinty tanks for shunting the Crook Street sidings, class 2 push-pull engines. There were about fifteen or sixteen locos.

Funniest thing was they got a new turntable just before the war that should have gone to Crescent Road but through an administrative mix-up went to Plodder Lane, a new 60ft turntable. I'll tell you where it was. At the side of Townley's Hospital is a walkway up to Plodder Lane and if you walk up that walkway today there is a bulge in the wall less than two hundred yards up because it was too big! I think that it was installed just before the war.

Bolton 26C had an electric turntable that was replaced with a vacuum one when the shed was renovated and redesigned in the early fifties.

We used to work from Bolton this Ancoats to Carlisle as far as Hellifield with an Austerity. Now at Low Moor Crossing at Clitheroe you wanted to get a run at 'em over the viaduct but at Whalley the signalman was always asleep and it was a level crossing so you had to stop. My mate, Big Wilf, gets fed up with this after a couple of nights so on the third night he didn't whistle, he crept up to the gates, got off the engine and crept up to the box and slid a window open. He put the clock forward an hour and woke him up and said, 'We've been here a bloody hour.' It was all panic then, ringing bells calling up the stations.'

MALCOLM FROST.

Malcolm Frost (Fireman) and Stanley Osborne (Driver) were returning light engine from Wigan to Bolton in the dark with No. 45378 at Crow Nest sidings. Stanley was wondering where he was you see. I said, 'We're in't loop Stanley'.

'Bloody Hell, we're not!' He hadn't realised that we had gone into the loop. So I said, 'Right, I'd better go back to the signalbox'. Then I realised. On trying to get off the engine, told him, 'We're up agin a stone wall!'

'Bloody Hell, we can't be!' was the reply.

'We are mate, there's a bridge there'. What had happened is that we had gone down the loop towards the headshunt at the end of the loop before it goes out onto the line. Well, we had gone straight down it an' smack into the side walls of a big overbridge. To get there we had demolished a big square salt box which were over four foot high, knocked buffers off the end and gone straight through a platelayers cabin made of sleepers and knocked two trees down, so our progress down that loop had been sort of eventful.

After we hit the bridge and they got a few lights on t' see, platelayer Cyril is stood wailing and moaning because his tea and sugar had been in't cabin. Thats all as he was bothered about, 'is tea and sugar.

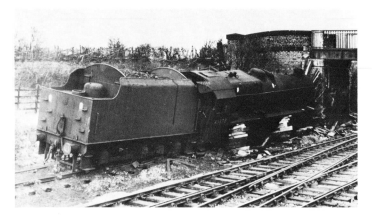

195. Crow Nest Junction, February 1965. The conclusion of overrunning the loop at Crow Nest, near Wigan, with 'Black Five' No.45378, and as described by Malcolm Frost above.

Photo: Dr. J. Gordon Blears

Harry Davies was firing on this Paignton to Accrington and then light engine to Newton Heath, so there were various ways you could come. They decided to come via Baxenden bank, Helmshore and Bury. Now they're coming into Helmshore under caution and there used to be a level crossing there and they came onto 'block' in the station. What the fireman had to do to follow rule 55 was walk through the crossing gates across the main road to reach the signalbox and sign the book. When he get there, there is no signalman so he thought, 'It's bloody queer that', so he comes back onto the platform and he can't find anybody about, no staff, nothing. Now just outside ther's a pub, so as a railway man, well, I' wonder if they'r in't pub', so he went into pub, asked landlord, 'Is there any of the station staff in here?'

'Who do you want?'

'Well, the signalman'.

'He's playing piano'.

'And the porter?'

'He's collecting glasses'.

So I goes up to this bloke at the piano and says, 'Are you the signalman?'

'Yes'.

'Well, we've got an engine waiting to come through the station and we're on the block'.

'Oh well, hang on a minute I'll just finish this tune'.

We worked the 3.50 to Liverpool then we used to work back to Wigan, book off light engine and back to Bolton before working Rochdale; later, we lost the Rochdale to a DMU so we just went back on shed from Wigan.

A Bolton engine came off (derailed) at down side box right underneath Moncrieff Street and at that time Moncrieff Street had been demolished bar for about six houses. This would be 1964/5. The tool van came off Bolton shed and in charge was Harry Burgess, Chargehand fitter, who weighed the situation up and decided to commandeer the station pilot to hook onto the front of this engine and try to pull it back on the road and so they put the packing underneath and said to the driver, 'When I give you the tip I want you both to open the regulator and we'll pull this engine back on'. It didn't work, both slipping on greasy rails. He then commandeered another engine, coupled that on and they all opened up and shuddered that much that somebody shouted on the platform, 'Whoa! Whoa!' and when they looked up he'd demolished all the bloody houses on Moncrieff Street. When the demolition men left on Friday night there had been just the shells, when they came back on Monday morning there was sod all!'

JIM MARKLAND.

Taking the Bullfield to Halliwell one morning in 1957 we were given twenty-seven all full coal wagons to go up the bank with. Our engine was No. 51498 and I was firing for Bill Hoggit. So when we have a load on like that we ask Bolton West signalbox to give us a good clear road right through Johnson Street fork and through Bradshawgate section, give us virtually right all the way to Halliwell. Old Bill was tall and deaf and he couldn't hear when he was thrashing it. So we set off and crept through the tunnels until we could site this (No. 43) distant and it was 'off'! The next one was just before we went into Bradshawgate tunnel, an upper quadrant one, and that was 'off' as well, so Bradshawgate had pulled his distant. Do you know, we screamed round that bend on three wheels, the firebox door was shut and I had put a pile on because I knew what Bill was like. You could hear all twenty-seven and the guards brake screaming as we went round that curve, we were bunker first and the exhaust hit the roof of the tunnel like a broadside of cannon and on the other side there was a 'Crab' with a bemused crew, warming up ready to bank us and we must have been doing in excess of thirty-five miles an hour when we passed them, which doesn't sound a lot, but with four foot six driving wheels you were cracking it and I actually put the brake on for the banker to join us at Craddock Lane box as Bill shouts, indignantly 'We could have swung 'em'.

We had a BR standard railmotor doing the Chorley trip, and in later years it ran between Horwich and Chorley. Coming back from Chorley the driver would be in the coach end and the fireman would be on his own.

You ran yourself round at Horwich. The station pilot in the afternoon would make its way to the points running onto Horwich works, go on and pick up a stores van. Sidings around Horwich Works were called 'The Jungle Shunt', 'On the Moss', 'Foundry Yard', 'Liverpool Road', 'Station Line', 'Paint Shop'. One section of line called the 'Board Side' was where engines were run up and down to see that the beat was right, and usually there would be three or four fitters on the footplate with an inspector for finished work area. He would say, 'Take 2976 and 'board side' it. You drop down to West Cabin and set back and you run up the boards at the top end of the works yard and then reverse back again'.

MIKE STRICKLETON.

Mike Strickleton is the nephew of Joe Strickleton with whom he shares an affinity for the footplate as a fireman. He remembers the filming of 'The Love Match' round Bolton in the 1950's and how they took No. 44311 to Skelmersdale to grease the rails to make it slip.

The cup match shown at Burnden in the film was between Charlton Athletic v the Wanderers.

Mike had a love match of his own when his courting style was rather cramped by his shift work and his fiance travelled with him, in the following train of course. One wintery trip to Blackpool with a Black Five the future Mrs Strickleton complained of the trains being cold so Mike put the train heating on full from the cab. The ploy had humourous side effects for upon it reaching Blackpool the staff at the station were amazed to see the train arrive full of overdressed business men from Manchester having discarded their overcoats and coats with the heat pouring out of the open carriage doors and half of the train asleep!

196. Fireman John Mather on the right in this 1930's view on the footplate of an ex-L&Y 2-4-2 tank. Hopefully, his experiences were better than those encountered on the Jubilee described earlier. *Photo: Courtesy John Mather*

197. Bolton Trinity Street, 15th April 1966. Malcolm Frost with Tommy Crook experiencing the last day of steam working from Bolton Shed on their Stanier 2-6-4T No.42252. The train is the 3.50p.m. all stations to Liverpool with the engine working back light. Sometimes the working was handled by a Class 5, as on the occasion of one coming into conflict with the bridge abutment at Crow Nest Junction. *Photo: Courtesy Malcolm Frost*

Acknowledgements.

The author would like to convey his appreciation to the following who have supplied information and helped him in numerous ways to compile this book:

The Editor & staff of the Bolton Evening News, B.D. Mills, and T.K. Campbell (Bolton Reference Library). Greg Fox, Terry Foley, Gordon Biddle, Frank Mullineux, Derek Ralphs, Kevin Ludlow, John Mather, Malcolm Frost, Joe Strickleton, Mike Strickleton, Tom Sibbering, Geoffery Webb, Jim Markland, John Hodgson (LYR Society), Steve Leyland, Chris Driver (Bolton Local History Museum), Neville Knight, Bill Rear.
The photographers and phototgraph collectors are acknowledged beneath each print but deserve special mention for their generosity here.

Other sources of reference:
The Lancashire & Yorkshire Railway (Three Vols.) by John Marshall, David & Charles.
The Railway Magazine, 1904.
The History of the Bolton & Leigh Railway by Lois Basnett.
The Railways of Bolton 1824–1959 by J.R. Bardsley.

Other titles by the Author
The Banbury to Verney Junction Branch (OPC) 1978.
Oxford to Cambridge (Vol. 1), Oxford to Bletchley (OPC) 1981.
Oxford to Cambridge (Vol. 2), Beltchley to Cambridge (OPC) 1983.
The Brill Tramway (OPC) 1985.
The Aylesbury Railway (OPC/Haynes) 1989.